T0194567

God's Final Answer To Job's Controversy:
—— The Leviathan ——

God's Final Answer To Job's Controversy:
The Leviathan

EDEM AMEYOU

WESTBOW
PRESS®
A DIVISION OF THOMAS NELSON
& ZONDERVAN

WestBow Press books may be ordered through booksellers or by contacting:

WestBow Press
A Division of Thomas Nelson & Zondervan
1663 Liberty Drive
Bloomington, IN 47403
www.westbowpress.com
1 (866) 928-1240

ISBN: 978-1-9736-4803-1 (sc)
ISBN: 978-1-9736-4805-5 (hc)
ISBN: 978-1-9736-4804-8 (e)

Library of Congress Control Number: 2018914490

Print information available on the last page.

WestBow Press rev. date: 12/12/2018

Contents

Foreword

The Book of Job has always been a difficult book to interpret. There are various theories on when and where and how the book was born, but now one has been able to give a final view on this. There are also different literal or symbolic interpretations of Job's message, but no one has come with one definitive exegesis of the book. Other ancient stories of an unfairly suffering man have been found, but they do not help interpret to book of Job. Furthermore, because the book of Job is so different from other Old Testament books, many find it challenging to interpret its meaning in line with general Biblical teaching.

Over the years I have read a few suggestions on the meaning of the Leviathan described at the end of the book of Job, but I have never come across the interpretation that Pastor Edem Ameyou gives in this book. He points to an eschatological dimension in the story of Job. This is a very interesting idea, and as we consider his view we are challenged to consider the evidence given, and we may also be provoked to weigh possible objections to his view. In short, all such contemplations are valuable, because they help us grow spiritually and lead us to understand the Bible better.

Kai Arasola
(Former Dean, Faculty of Religious Studies
Asia-Pacific International University-Thailand)

Thanks and Apreciation

Special thanks to:

- Lydia Lassey (Togo)
- Pirjo Riikonen (Finland)
- Ron Clark (Illinois – USA)
- Joel Mahoro (Manila - Philippines)
- Roger Mathias (Guadeloupe)
- Martynas Baltiejus (Finland)
- Zo Misaina Voaharinoferana (Finland)

This book is specially dedicated to all my brothers and sisters in Christ around the world who love our Lord Jesus- Christ, and long for His soon appearing .

Preface

The book of Job, possibly the oldest part of the Bible according to the Judeo-Christian tradition (Morris, 2000) (Ross, 2014), reveals the great controversy between good and evil. From its very beginning, there is a discussion between Satan and the God of heaven regarding the life of Job and the issue of worship. Job went through terrible calamities and persecutions no human being on earth ever went through; he lost his children, his friends, his belongings. In his trials, he turned to God for an answer. God's silence seemed to be such an eternity for the patriarch; but God finally came in a whirlwind to answer him with various elements of nature, as nature was the opened book in the old times which instructed men on wisdom (Genesis 49).

God's final words for Job rested upon a strange, wild animal that is commonly portrayed by some humans as the dragon or the devil, but by others as a harmless sea creature: The Leviathan. This beast has different symbolical meanings in various passages of the Bible. Based on the content of the 41st chapter of the book of Job, it seemed that God used this figure to teach Job some lessons of uprightness, strength, and surrender. Why a Leviathan? What does it represent in Job 41? Could this be Satan?

Of Lucifer before the fall, God said: "...You were the seal of perfection, full of wisdom and perfect in beauty. You were in Eden, the garden of God; every precious stone was your covering: the sardius, topaz, and diamond, Beryl, onyx, and jasper, sapphire, turquoise, and emerald with gold. The workmanship of your timbrels and pipes was prepared for you on the day you were created. "You were the anointed cherub who covers; I established you; you were on the holy mountain of God; you walked back and forth in the midst of fiery stones. You were perfect in your ways from the day you were created, till iniquity was found in you (Ezekiel 28 :12-15)"-NKJV.

After his fall, no praise was ever given to Satan by God, but instead the following names all over the Bible to warn Man he is the author of sin and destruction: he is called the father of lie, the accuser of the brethren, the dragon, the adversary, the angel of the abyss, the god of this world, the devil, the impure spirit, the enemy, the mercenary, the murderer, the prince of the power of the air, the prince of the world of darkness, the tempter, the seducer, the serpent.

If God never praised Satan after his fall from glory, but spoke of his perfection only before the fall, His final words in Job's controversy suggests that:

- God was not spending so much time to talk about his enemy or render a praise-like speech about Satan to His servant Job.
- God was not talking about Satan to Job in his most difficult time.
- God was not asking Job a contemplative exercise of Satan when Job was in search of the most important answer for his life's controversy.

For instance, when Israel was in trouble, God pointed them to the Passover Lamb; when Man was in sin, God pointed him to Calvary; there he beheld the Lamb of God, and learned the importance of self-denial and love. In our troubles, God always has the best answers that can satisfy our questionings. Job answered God: "I know that You can do everything, and that no purpose of Yours can be withheld from You. You asked, 'Who is this who hides counsel without knowledge?' Therefore I have uttered what I did not understand, things too wonderful for me, which I did not know (Job 42 verses 2-3-NKJV). Job then understood, these things too wonderful for him. So if the Leviathan of Job 41, does not refer to the dragon, or Satan, what could be the meaning of God's final words to Job's controversy in the symbolism of this awful beast?

God bless you as you get closer to Him by the reading of this book. Edem Ameyou (Pastor)

The Great Controversy

In Revelation 12:7 (NKJV) is told the story of the great controversy between Christ and Satan.

> And war broke out in heaven: Michael and his angels fought with the dragon; and the dragon and his angels fought, but they did not prevail, nor was a place found for them in heaven any longer. So the great dragon was cast out, that serpent of old, called the Devil and Satan, who deceives the whole world; he was cast to the earth, and his angels were cast out with him.
>
> Evil originated with Lucifer, who rebelled against the government of God. Before his fall, Lucifer was a covering cherub, distinguished by his excellence. God made him good and beautiful, as near as possible like himself.[1]

Jesus Christ is the essence of the Father; He is God. Lucifer, on the other hand, was created by God, but he is not the essence of God; he is God's creature.

> He glorified in his brightness and exaltation and aspired to be equal with God. He was beloved and reverenced by the heavenly hosts; angels delighted to execute his commands, and he was clothed with wisdom and glory

above them all. Yet the Son of God was exalted above him, as one in power and authority with the Father.[2]

Because Lucifer did not want to worship Christ and instead wanted to take His place, he was cast out of heaven.

> How you have fallen from heaven, morning star, son of the dawn! You have been cast down to the earth, you who once laid low the nations! (Isaiah 14:12 NIV)

So to the inhabitants of earth, God said,

> Therefore rejoice, you heavens and you who dwell in them! But woe to the earth and the sea, because the devil has gone down to you! He is filled with fury, because he knows that his time is short. (Revelation 12:12 NIV)

Ever since, the earth has been the battlefield of the great controversy between Christ and Satan, and human life has become the center of the battle. The life of Job is the perfect example the Bible gives us about this fight. God bragged about Job's faithfulness to Him. Satan wished to witness this obedience, especially in the most difficult times of Job's life. God allowed him to stripe Job of everything important he had in life, but Job was still faithful to God.

> Though He slay me, yet will I trust Him. Even so, I will defend my own ways before Him. (Job 13:15 NKJV)

The greatest concern in this battle is humankind's response. If in our trying times we fail to remain faithful to God, of course His name will not be glorified. But if in every situation—good or bad—we give glory to God as Job did, the manifestation of His power in our lives will be a testimony to the fallen world and to the whole universe. Such manifestation of God's power in Job's life was most visible in the trying times of his life. Remember that Satan's accusation against God was that Job worshipped Him because he was blessed. For that reason, God allowed him to take away everything that belonged to Job except his life.

So the question is this: on earth, will there be somebody like Job who is faithful and enduring in suffering and is able to stand, especially in the end times controversy, to vindicate God's character?

There are at least two answers Job sought for: the reason why he suffered and the meaning of those sufferings for him, a servant of God. God's final answer for him was the Leviathan. If the Leviathan is the allegorical answer God gave to Job regarding the reason and meaning of his suffering, then Job might have been acquainted with that figure in his time. And its symbolism might have an important spiritual significance in the great controversy. So it is important to find out what that symbol means, what Job knew about it in his time, and how it relates to the issue of worship in the great controversy between Christ and Satan.

Job and the Leviathan

God created humans, so He might share His life and glory with them. In His creation is revealed His self-giving and self-sacrificing love. From God comes our joy, life, peace, and happiness. So to survive, humans need to be connected to Him.

Because Job worshipped God, his faith was tested. In his life, worship meant trust and obedience even in the midst of adversity. He suffered for his uprightness and abiding faith in God. His life tells us that suffering reveals our true character. If we are connected to God, and if He is in charge of our life, His life will be seen in us, His love will shine in the midst of our darkness, and we will come out triumphant from our trials. As God invited Job to ponder on the attributes of the Leviathan (Job 40:24–32, 41:1–24) for an answer, this question remains: what does the Leviathan have to do with Job's controversy or with the controversy between good and evil?

The Hebrew Word "Leviathan" in Job 41

In biblical times, nature in general and animals especially were used to teach men wisdom.

> But ask the animals, and they will teach you, or the birds
> in the sky, and they will tell you. (Job 12:7 NIV)

Good attributes of animals were used for the description of good character types, while their bad attributes were used for the description of bad character types.

- In Genesis 49, Jacob pronounced the prophetical blessings on his twelve children by using animal symbolism.
- In Revelation 5:5, Jesus is called the Lion of the tribe of Judah in reference to the mighty work of redemption, but in 1 Peter 5:8, Satan is identified as a roaring lion searching for whom he may devour.
- In Isaiah 40:31, those who wait upon the Lord are identified as powerful eagles, but in Leviticus 11:13, the eagle is considered an impure and detestable bird.

The Leviathan, in the Bible, represents good or bad attributes, depending on the context in which it is used. It does not have a clear-cut definition throughout the Bible. It differs from one passage to the other.

- In Psalm 104:25–26, it speaks of the power of God in creation.
- In Psalm 74, some scholars agree that it refers to Egypt and its pharaoh, the king of Egypt.[3, 4] In the same psalm, it is believed

by others to be a seven-headed beast familiar in the days of the psalmist.[5]

- In Isaiah 27:1, some scholars believe it may signify the dragon, or the devil himself, who will be destroyed in the end times.[6,7]
- In Job 41, some call it a gigantic beast or a sea monster.[8]

Some other Bible scholars believed it is either a crocodile or a whale. In psalms 104 and 74, for example, it lives in the sea, which means it could probably be a whale, a great sea animal that was well known in the time of Moses (Genesis 1:21) and Job. Parkhurst, borrowing from the nature of land serpent and fish, said the Leviathan would be a crocodile that lives under the water and on the shore. He said,

> And all that can be said to solve these difficulties is that there are many different species of whales, several that are known, and probably many more that are not known; and that although this description, in all its parts, may not exactly suit any species of them which we know, there may be others in the immense ocean with which we are not acquainted that it may suit; creatures which, though comprehended under the general name of whales, may, in many respects, be very different from, and much larger than, any that have been taken.

It is well possible that Job may have known about these whales.

The Leviathan in Job 41

Among the many views of scholars regarding the meaning of the Leviathan in Job 41, Matthew Henry's 1706 commentary sided with Richard Blackmore, who believed the Leviathan could not be the Behemoth, as some believed, as the Behemoth could have been the elephant. So the meaning of *Behemoth* in the former chapter as an elephant or hippopotamus would have nothing to do with the nature of the Leviathan in Job 41.

J. Campbell said in 1738,

as the true signification of Behemoth has been much controversed, so also great disputes have arisen concerning the import of this word Leviathan; some conceiving it as intended of the whale, others of the crocodile. Both these creatures are so well known, that a description of them will be both superfluous and tedious. The learned Mr. Pool in his Annotations and in his Synopsis, has laid before his readers variety of proofs, tending to shew, that the Word of God in the book of Job are fulfilled, in case the Leviathan should be taken as either, tho´ we are inclined from various reasons to believe it is rather to be understood of the crocodile. Because it is reasonable to suppose that the Almighty would choose no animal for his demonstration of his power and wisdom, but what was sufficiently known to Job and his friends; otherwise the arguments raised therefrom would evidently have less weights. Now, the whale could not be a creature so known, whereas the crocodile being common in Egypt, they could not be acquainted therewith, and with all its properties.

The Leviathan is here said to have had large and strong knit scales as if they have been sealed together, whereas the whale has no scale at all; but the crocodile corresponds exactly to that description.

His breath is set forth as very hot, and that by the strongest metaphors; which has been observed of the last mentioned animal, but never in whales or in any other fishes.

In his commentary, Matthew Henry (1706) also agreed with Bochart and Poole who believe the Leviathan could rather be the crocodile well known in the Egyptian river.

(Gill J., Commentary of Job 41:1, 1999) in the context of Job includes river in the expression of sea which could solve the biblical problem; that crocodile was only found in rivers.

Gerety (2018) said in his book *"crocodiles and humans have seldom gotten on well. Historians have theorized that the fearsome Leviathan, imagined as a whale ever since Moby Dick, and described at length in the book of Job is in fact a crocodile"*

The King James Version of the Bible also refers to the Leviathan in a footnote to Job 41:1 as a crocodile. (Giblett, 2009).

Also, in the Revised Standard Version of the Bible, the Leviathan is mentioned as a crocodile in the footnote to Job 40:15- 22 (Giblett, 2009). Even though all Christian scholars do not agree on a single identity of the Leviathan, some of them have concluded that the crocodile best fits its nature in Job 41.

Building on the findings of these scholars that the Leviathan in Job 41 would refer to the crocodile that would have been well known by the patriarch Job in his time, here is a comparative between the characteristics of the crocodile and those of the Leviathan of Job chapter 41.

CROCODILE	LEVIATHAN IN JOB 41
Skin Texture	
- "Beneath its scaly sheath and craggy osteoderms is another layer of armor, built of rows of bony overlapping shingles, or osteoscutes, that are both strong and flexible. - And beneath that formidable barrier is an immune system that merits the modifier: it is virtually immune to defeat. (Natalie Angier, 2004) - small caliber bullets cannot penetrate a crocodile skin. (Hays, 2008)	Can you fill his skin with harpoons (Job 41:7)-NIV? Who can remove his outer coat? Who can approach him with a double bridle? (Job 41:13)-NIV. The arrow cannot make him flee; Sling stones become like stubble to him. Darts are regarded as straw; He laughs at the threat of javelins. (Job 41:28 – 29)-NIV

Skin Texture	
The body armature, scutes, shield and scales are often regarded as protective devices during internecine battles (Sherstha, 2001) 	When he raises himself up, the mighty are afraid; Because of his crashing they are beside themselves. Lay your hand on him; Remember the battle Never do it again! Job 41:25-NIV I will not conceal his limbs, His mighty power, or his graceful proportions. – (Job 41:12)-NIV

Plate Unity in Skin Texture	
He has a thick skin composed of close-set overlapping bony plates (Alligator) 	His rows of scales are his pride, shut up tightly as with a seal; -One is so near another that no air can come between them; - They are joined one to another, -They stick together and cannot be parted (Job 41:15 -17)-NIV; -The folds of his flesh are joined together; They are firm on him and cannot be moved. (Job 41:23)-NIV.

Strength	
Crocodiles can submerge and remain underwater for a variety of reasons. In most voluntary dives, crocodiles stay underwater for between 10 to 15 minutes. If the crocodile is trying to hide from a threat, dive length may be longer, up to 30 minutes or more. Most crocodiles can actually remain underwater up to 2 hours if pressed (Britton, 2012). (crocodilian biology database)	Can you draw out Leviathan with a hook? Or snare his tongue with a line which you lower? Can you put a reed through his nose? Or pierce his jaw with a hook? Will he make many supplications to you? Will he speak softly to you? Will he make a covenant with you? *(emphasis Psalm 50:1- 4)*
-Just because you can't see a crocodile doesn't mean there is not one close by. Crocodiles can be very patient and can stay underwater and unseen for up to four hours without even a breath. (Be (Crocwise)	Will you take him as a servant forever? Will you play with him as with a bird? Or will you leash him for your maidens? Will your companions make a banquet of him? Will they apportion him among the merchants? (Job 41:1-6)-NIV
If there is no food available, they are able to survive for over a year without eating. They seem to shut down and live off their own fat and muscle reserves until they manage to find food again. (Team, 2014)	Who can open the doors of his face, *With* his terrible teeth all around? Job 41:14-NIV
they can go without food for as long as three years (Cam, 2014)	Indeed, any hope of overcoming him is false; Shall one not be overwhelmed at the sight of him? No one is so fierce that he would dare stir him up.

Strength	
Crocodiles can go for years without eating anything. Despite their reputation as ferocious carnivores, crocodiles don't actually need to eat regularly to survive. (Team A. A., 2014).	Who then is able to stand against Me? Who has preceded Me, that I should pay him? Everything under heaven is Mine. (Job 41: 9 – 11)-NIV.

Countenance	
the "crocodile, with its armature of scale rind, and formidable jaws beset with bristling teeth, need fear nothing short of a rifle-bullet". - The Edinburg Review of Critical Journal-(1844) . 	His sneezing's flashes forth light, and his eyes are like the eyelids of the morning. Out of his mouth go burning lights; Sparks of fire shoot out. Smoke goes out of his nostrils, as from a boiling pot and burning rushes. His breath kindles coals, and a flame goes out of his mouth. Strength dwells in his neck, And sorrow dances before him. (Job 41: 18-22)-NIV.

Influence	
He maketh a path to shine after him—Houbigant (2011) renders the text, He leaves behind him a shining path; that is, the way in which he moves appears shining and conspicuous, as when a ship sails, and leaves a visible path behind it, which in the night appears to shine."	His undersides are like sharp potsherds; He spreads pointed marks in the mire. He makes the deep boil like a pot; He makes the sea like a pot of ointment. He leaves a shining wake behind him;

Influence	
	One would think the deep had white hair. On earth there is nothing like him, Which is made without fear- **Job 41: 30-33-NI**V

So, in Job 41, the Leviathan is personalized, and in the symbolisms that appear, the characteristics of the crocodile that could be noticed in his description are the texture of the skin, the plates unity in the skin texture, the inner strength, the countenance and the influence:

- The crocodile has a strong skin that serves as a heavy coat; in Job 41 likewise, the Leviathan has a heavy coat which protects his body.
- The structure of the crocodile skin is a composition of close-set overlapping bony plates. In Job 41 the bony plates of the Leviathan are rows of scales that stick together and cannot be separated.
- In difficult times crocodiles are patient creatures which can stay under water for many hours, even without a breath, and go without food up to three years; in Job 41, the Leviathan is identified to a resistant creature which is not easily made a prey.
- The crocodile leaves a shiny path behind its when it moves in the water. In Job 41, the Leviathan leaves a shining wave behind him.

On the other hand, without reference to Job 41 or the character of the Leviathan, Ellen. G. White, referring to the Great Controversy, wrote various documents about the end times believers who will vindicate the character of Christ during the Jacob´s time of trouble. A close study of some of her statements reveals a parallelism between her writings and the description of the characteristics of the Leviathan in Job chapter 41.

Skin Texture (Coat)	
LEVIATHAN IN JOB 41	**PEOPLE OF GOD IN TIME OF TROUBLE**
Can you fill his skin with harpoons (Job 41:7)? Who can remove his outer coat? Who can approach him with a double bridle? (Job 41:13)-NIV.	-It was a covering that God was drawing over His people to protect them in the time of trouble, and every soul that has decided on the truth and was pure in heart was to be covered with the covering of the Almighty- (White, 1945) At our happy, holy state the wicked were enraged, and would rush violently up to lay hands on us to thrust us into prison, when we would stretch forth the hand in the name of the Lord, and they would fall helpless to the ground ... And they were all clothed with a glorious white mantle from their shoulders to their feet ..." (White, 1945)

Plate Unity in Skin Texture	
His rows of scales are his pride, Shut up tightly as with a seal; -One is so near another that no air can come between them; - They are joined one to another, -They stick together and cannot be parted (Job 41:15 -17)-NIV;	"...Here on the sea of glass the 144,000 stood in a perfect square – (White, 1945) The 144,000 were all sealed, and perfectly united. On their foreheads was written, "God, New Jerusalem," and a glorious star containing Jesus' new name - (White, 1945).

Plate Unity in Skin Texture	
They are brothers who embrace each other, seize each other, remain inseparable (Job 41:15-17-, 2010)-(Second) -The folds of his flesh are joined together; They are firm on him and cannot be moved. (Job 41:23)-NIV.	

Strength	
Can you draw out Leviathan with a hook? Or snare his tongue with a line which you lower? Can you put a reed through his nose? Or pierce his jaw with a hook? Will he make many supplications to you? Will he speak softly to you? Will he make a covenant with you? *(emphasis Psalm 50:1- 4)* Will you take him as a servant forever? Will you play with him as with a bird? Or will you leash him for your maidens? Will your companions make a banquet of him? Will they apportion him among the merchants? (Job 41:1-6)-NIV	In the midst of the time of trouble- trouble such as has not been since there was a nation, - His chosen ones will stand unmoved (White E. G., Prophets and Kings, 1943). But in the midst of the time such as has not been since there was a nation, God's chosen people will stand unmoved – Testimonies to The Church Vol 9 (White, 2011) Though enemies may thrust them into prison, yet dungeon walls cannot cut off the communication between their souls and Christ (White E., 1990)

Strength

Who can open the
doors of his face,
With his terrible teeth all
around? (Job 41:14)-NIV

Indeed, any hope of
overcoming him is false;
Shall one not be overwhelmed
at the sight of him?
No one is so fierce that he
would dare stir him up.
Who then is able to
stand against Me?
Who has preceded Me,
that I should pay him?
Everything under heaven is
Mine. (Job 41: 9 – 11)-NIV.

The arrow cannot make him
flee; Sling stones become
like stubble to him.
Darts are regarded as straw;
He laughs at the
threat of javelins.
(Job 41:28 – 29)-NIV

When he raises himself up,
the mighty are afraid;
Because of his crashing they
are beside themselves.
Lay your hand on him;
Remember the battle—
Never do it again!
(Job 41:8)-NIV

- In the time of trouble, we all
fled from the cities and village,
but were pursued by the wicked,
who entered the houses of
the saints with a sword. They
raised the sword to kill us,
but it broke and fell powerless
as a straw. (White, 1945)

Countenance	
His sneezing's flashes forth light, And his eyes are like the eyelids of the morning. Out of his mouth go burning lights; Sparks of fire shoot out. Smoke goes out of his nostrils, as from a boiling pot and burning rushes. His breath kindles coals, and a flame goes out of his mouth. Strength dwells in his neck, And sorrow dances before him. (Job 41: 18-22-NIV.	Their countenance is lighted up with glory and shine as did the face of Moses when he came down from Sinai. The wicked cannot look upon them- (White E., 1990) 

Influence	
His undersides are like sharp potsherds; He spreads pointed marks in the mire. He makes the deep boil like a pot; He makes the sea like a pot of ointment.	They bore the signet of heaven. They reflected the image of God. They were full of the light and the glory of the Holy One (White, 1889).
He leaves a shining wake behind him; One would think the deep had white hair. On earth there is nothing like him, Which is made without fear- **Job 41: 30-33-NIV**	

In Job 41, the Leviathan has a strong coat of protection that makes his pride; in the writings of Ellen White, the saints living at the return of Jesus, or 144,000 will be protected by God's glorious covering from their shoulders to their feet. For memory, the life of Job likewise was protected by God before his life calamities (Job 2:6).

In Job 41:15-17, his rows of scales are his pride, shut up tightly as with a seal; these rows of scales are interpreted by Second (2010) as "brothers who embrace each other, seize each other, and remain inseparable; regarding the 144,000 or living saints in the end time conflict, Ellen White wrote they were sealed and perfectly united.

In Job 41, the Leviathan is not an easy prey; talking about the same group of people, Ellen White wrote in the time of trouble, they will stand unmoved and nothing can cut their communication with God.

In Job 41, the Leviathan is a fiery creature; talking about the saints in time of trouble, Ellen White wrote their countenance is lighted up with the glory of God.

In job 41, he leaves a shiny path behind him; of the end time saints, Ellen White wrote, they are full of the glory and light of God.

According to the Joseph Benson commentary, (1857), more often, when talking about the Leviathan, only the original non-translated term is mentioned; Leviathan being the transliteration of the Hebrew original word; but when the Old Testament was translated into Greek, the word dragon was used instead of Leviathan; but this still does not satisfy the real meaning of the original word. In his commentary about Job 41, Gill J (1999) said:

-    it is not easy to say "Leviathan" is a compound word:
of *"than"* the first syllable of *"thanni"*, rendered either a whale, or a dragon, or a serpent; and of *"levi"*, which signifies conjunction, from the close joining of its scales, Job 41:15; the patriarch Levi had his name from the same word; see Genesis 29:34".

In the context of Job 41, it is important to consider the meaning of the two roots words *"thannin"* and *"Levi"*.

The word *"thannin"* in the transliterated word Leviathan did not only mean dragon, large serpent, but was rendered also as a whale; the same word is used for crocodile in Ezekiel 29:3-4 and Ezekiel 32:3. As believed by some scholars, *"thanni"* referred to the crocodile in Job 41, a fearless beast, which has a strong coat or a thick skin composed of bone set overlapping together which cannot be separated; this denotes a certain physical unity and order.

The word *"thannin"* meaning fish, dragon, or a large serpent), and literally used for land serpent and couple dragon is the solid argument Bochart and Poole used to support their claim that the Leviathan refers to the crocodile which lives only in the river, since the Bible did not make mention that the Leviathan lives in the sea; (*"thannin"* parallel with Leviathan and used for crocodile in Ezekiel 29:3-4 and Ezekiel 32:3).

The other part of the root word in Leviathan to be considered is the word *"Levi"*.

In the Bible, talking about Lea the first wife of Jacob in Genesis 29:34-NIV, the Bible said: "Again she conceived, and when she gave birth to a son she said, "Now at last my husband will become attached to me, because I have borne him three sons." So he was named "Levi". The name Levi "לֵוִי" is a proper name, masculine which means dubious, joined (like in Genesis 39:24) or attached to; (Brown F., 1906). When pronouncing the prophetical blessings over his children in Genesis 49, Jacob said: "Simeon and Levi are brothers; instruments of cruelty are in their dwelling place. Let not my soul enter their council; Let not my honor be united to their assembly; for in their anger they slew a man, and in their self-will, they hamstrung an ox. Cursed be their anger, for it is fierce; And their wrath, for it is cruel! I will divide them in Jacob and scatter them in Israel".(Genesis 49:5 – 7-NKJV). That does not sound like a good blessing, but rather like a curse; (for memory, Levi was the Son of Lea who murdered an entire town with his brother to avenge their sister Dina who was defiled (Genesis 34:25). During the apostasy of Israel, their curse was turned into a blessing; they were the people who remained faithful to God when Israel went away to build the golden calf; their faithfulness granted them the honor of receiving the priestly status (Ginzberg, 1909); they did not receive any land or earthly inheritance in the territory of Canaan (Joshua 13:33.), neither were they numbered among the Jewish census, but they were the closest to the sanctuary of God, their camp was the symbol of holiness and consecration to God; according to Charles (1913), they were separately counted as God's special army ; their curse opened the priesthood to members of other tribes; and their tribe became a special, distinct tribe (Matthew Black, 1962); they were dedicated to God's service in the sanctuary, always ready for sacrifice; as long as the cause was to defend the name of God (Numbers 18:2 – 4; Exodus 32:26 – 29; Genesis 49; Exodus 2:11 -15;

Numbers 25:6–13). Their tribe was responsible for religious leadership (Waters), and for the daily sacrifices of animals in the sanctuary service. Regarding this, Farbiaz (2009) said they were perhaps chosen precisely because "they straddled holiness and violence, purity and power" .

In response to Job´s questioning in Job 41, there is no rebuke given to this Leviathan; but instead, God used it to teach Job lessons of surrender and total trust in Him and dependence in adversity.

Even though without a clear definition of the identity of the Leviathan, there are some references about the role it played in the Old Testament during the Exodus of Israel from Egypt (Psalm 74 verse 14), and also some references in Judaism regarding it supposed role in the life of God´s righteous children, in the end times.

In Psalm 74:14 for example, it is said that its head was broken, and given for food for the children of God; this is a symbolism of its supposed role in the deliverance of God´s people. About that verse, Coffman (1999) wrote: "This does not mean that Israel fed, literally, upon the bodies of Pharaoh's army washed ashore, but that Israel was armed with the weapons of the destroyed enemy".

In the New Testament for example, Jesus said in John 4:34-NKJV, "My food is to do the will of Him who sent Me, and to finish His work". In this passage also, food is not to be taken literally, but as a reference to the earnest desire of Jesus to do His Father´s will. Whether in this passage of John 4:34 or in Psalm 74:14, food has the connotation of assimilation.

In Judaism also, where some references to the role of the Leviathan in the life of God´s end-times children are spoken about, there is still this notion of food. According to Pieter Willem, (1999), the body of the Leviathan will be "reserved for the banquet that will be given to the righteous children of God" on the advent of the Messiah.

In Job 41:6-NKJV, it is written: "Will your companions make a banquet of him? Will they apportion him among the merchants?". Added to this notion of food in the *"Talmud Baba Bathra 75a"* (third of the "three tractates in the Talmud that deals with a person's responsibilities and rights as the owner of property"), (Finkel, 1993) wrote that the skin of the Leviathan would serve as a covering of the tent where the banquet of God would take place; that citation goes like this: "May it be Your will, Lord our God and God of our forefathers, that just as I have fulfilled and dwelt in this sukkah, so may I merit in the coming year to dwell in the sukkah of the skin of Leviathan. Next year in Jerusalem".

All these tell us that the characteristics of the Leviathan and its skin or coat have important theological meanings or significance in the life of God´s end-time righteous children.

The commonality between Psalm 74:14, these Judaic references, and the findings in the two tables above, are the following:

-   The righteousness of God´s children;
-   A coat of protection;
-   The time when the Messiah will return for a banquet;
-   And the end of a final conflict.

In the Bible, the parable of the wedding banquet is found in Matthew 22: 1-14. The prophet Isaiah, and John the apostle made a reference to the same event in the following terms:

-   I delight greatly in the LORD; my soul rejoices in my God. For he has clothed me with garments of salvation and arrayed me in a robe of his righteousness, as a bridegroom adorns his head like a priest, and as a bride adorns herself with her jewels (Isaiah 61:10-NIV).
-   Let us rejoice and be glad and give Him glory! For the wedding of the Lamb has come, and his bride has made herself ready. Fine linen, bright and clean, was given her to wear." (Fine linen stands for the righteous acts of God's holy people)-(Revelation 19:8-NIV).

As this could be noticed, the notion of banquet in the New Testament Bible is often linked to the robe of righteousness; all these three Bible references above refer to the spiritual preparation of God´s righteous children, and their readiness before the return of Jesus-Christ.

The conclusion that can be drawn from these findings, is that while Job was questioning the controversy between good and evil, and how his trials will end, God answered him by pointing him to a group of people who will stand like him in the end of times; they will be ready and wrapped up in His righteousness, sealed or sheltered like him and the children of Israel at Passover before the final destruction; God´s righteousness on them will be figuratively as strong as the coat of a Leviathan; they will be closely united to each other as the bony plates of the skin of the Leviathan; their holy influence and countenance and their faith in God will be as strong as the character of a Leviathan during the time of trouble that will come upon the earth; they are a type of the united tribe of Levi who served God day and night in the temple; they are the sons of righteousness; they are the sons of God that the whole universe is waiting to see manifested; they are those who would have overcome pride and will be kings over all the children of pride; they are those who will make a covenant with God through sacrifice (Psalm 50:5-6); they are those who will vindicate God´s character on earth in answer to the great controversy between God and Satan. Those people are the ones called the 144,000 :

- And I heard the number of them which were sealed: and there were sealed a hundred and forty and four thousand of all the tribes of the children of Israel (Revelation 7:4-KJV)
- Then I looked, and there before me was the Lamb, standing on Mount Zion, and with him 144,000 who had His name and His Father's name written on their foreheads (Revelation 14:1-NIV).

It is not clear in the book of Job that Job himself knew God has chosen him to vindicate His character; but God knew he could; the Bible only told us that God asked Satan: "have you considered my servant Job? In other words, God told Satan He had a witness He can trust, a witness who can glorify Him, worship Him and vindicate His character in any situation. Many of the sufferings children of God go through are for the purpose of vindicating the character and name of God; for that reason we should not murmur, but let God do His work in us. It seems that Job did not quite understand what was happening to him. In this, the concluding words of God to Him are to be taken seriously: "Who is this that obscures my plan with words without knowledge?"(Job 38:2)-NIV.

Many a time in the Bible, when faithful servants of God are asking questions about their tribulations, God gives them the answer by pointing them to an antitype that best explain their situation, an antitype which is more than enough to satisfy their queries.

For example:

- When Elijah the prophet was depressed and afraid to be killed by Jezebel, God told him he had 7000 more prophets who had never bowed down to Baal; God pointed Elijah to other faithful servants of Him to come (1 King 19: 1- 18).
- When Adam sinned against God and began to accuse his wife, God pointed him to Jesus Christ the ultimate Savior of the human race (Genesis 3:15; 21).
- When Moses prayed to God to let him enter the promised Land, God refused him to, but he beheld in vision the holy city of God, which God let him enter (Deuteronomy1:37; Matthew 17:1 – 13).
- When Abraham asked God about the lamb, he was provided a lamb for the sacrifice; that lamb represented Christ who will come to save the world (Genesis 22:8; John 1:29).

Many of the Old Testament patriarchs did not receive an answer; they died in faith, not having received the promises, nor witnessed the antitypes of the answers they were looking for"; but God gave them a vision of those antitypes; they saw them afar off and were assured of them; as it is said in Hebrews 11:13-NIV, "they only saw them and welcomed them from a distance, admitting that they were foreigners and strangers on earth".

God's servants	Quests	God answer
Adam	Trouble about his future after sin	I will put enmity between you and the serpent (Genesis 3:15)
Abraham	Trouble about the lamb for sacrifice	God will provide Himself a Lamb (John 1:7)
Elijah	Trouble about his persecution	The 7000 prophets who did not bow to Baal (1 King 19:18)

God's servants	Quests	God answer
Moses	Trouble about the earthly Canaan	God received him in the heavenly Canaan (Matthew 17)
Job	Trouble about his persecution	The Leviathan: The 144,000 (Job 41)

When Job got this answer of the Leviathan from God in the 41st chapter, he then understood what was happening to him; he was fully satisfied, he repented. Moreover, he saw the great picture beyond his life; he was blessed to have a glimpse of the end of the great controversy between good and evil; through God's speech, he beheld in vision the glorious army of God of the end times: the 144,000; things indeed too wonderful to behold(Job 42:3).

Characteristics of the Leviathan

The Levites in the Old Testament can give us an idea about who the 144,000 or Leviathan of Job 41 is; because the Leviathan is a type of that tribe of Levi.

The Levites were scattered among the twelve tribes of Israel (Jacob in blessing Levi said, "I will divide them in Jacob and scatter them in Israel"(Genesis 49:5 – 7); their name seems to be a descriptive attribute for people *"particularly suited to the priesthood"* (Singer, Jewish Encylopedia, 1907); they did not have a possession in Israel neither were they numbered during the count of the people; they were numbered separately as a special army (Ginzberg, 1909). According to Joshua 13:33, the Lord God was their inheritance; because of their faithfulness to God, they were honored by God to receive the priestly status (Ginzberg, 1909); they lived a consecrated life to God by working daily in the sanctuary; their priesthood "was originally open to any tribe, but gradually became seen as a distinct tribe to themselves" (Matthew Black, 1962).

Likewise, the Bible said of the 144,000 that they are:

From the twelve tribes of Israel: Looking back into the prophetical blessing of the children of Israel, in Genesis 45, Jacob blessed his twelve children who all have different character types. According to their birth order, Jacob's children were: Ruben, Simeon, Levi, Judah, Dan, Naphtali, Gad, Aser, Issachar, Zebulon, Joseph, and Benjamin. Later in the Scriptures, the Levites were put in charge of the Tabernacle of God (Numbers 1:47 – 54), and Joseph's inheritance was given to his sons Ephraim and Manasseh (Numbers 2:1 – 34). From a study conducted by the late Leslie Hardinge (2012), the human characters of the twelve children of Israel could be classified as followed based on the instruction given to God by Moses:

TRIBES	STONES	EMBLEMS	NATURAL CHARACTERS
Judah	Carnelian	Lion	Independent
Issachar	Peridot	Sun	Complacent
Zebulon	Emerald	Ship	Wanderer
Ruben	Ruby	Man	Sensual
Simeon	Sapphire	Citadel	Aggressive
Gad	Sardonyx	Troop	Warrior
Ephraim	Orange	Ox	Brilliant
Manasseh	Zircon	Unicorn	Shrinking
Benjamin	Amethyst	Horse	Tenacious
Dan	Topaz	Eagle	Judging
Asher	Onyx	Tree	Prosperous
Naphtali	Plasma	Deer	Wise

The leaders on the East were Judah (independent), Issachar (complacent), Zebulon (wanderer). The carnals on the South were Ruben (sensual), Simeon (aggressive), Gad (Warrior).The hard workers on the West were Ephraim (brilliant), Manasseh (shrinking), Benjamin (tenacious). The complacent or those who could be called today free spirit on the north were Dan (judging), Asher (prosperous), Naphtali (wise).

Dan on the other hand is not mentioned among the 144,000 in the book of Revelation. Dan in Hebrew means to judge (Gill, 1999); the critical spirit and back biting which causes division among brothers did not allow Dan such privilege; this was a character like the one of Lucifer, dividing the angels and misrepresenting God's character in heaven and in the garden of Eden; Dan was not wholly consecrated to God and was involved in idols worship (2 Kings 18: 28 -30; 1 Chronicles 2 - 10). Dan was simply replaced by Levi the murderer who repented, and gave himself wholly to God and by grace became a faithful servant in the sanctuary of God; in his mouth no words of deceit were found, no back biting between brothers, but love and unity instead. So Dan is not among the 144,000.

The tribe of Ephraim likewise was replaced by the tribe of Joseph his father. The name Ephraim in Hebrew means double ash-heap, doubly fruitful ("fruitful"; Genesis 41:52; 49:22). His name matches that of his father Joseph (Genesis 49:22). But because of his idolatry (Hosea 4:17), he was replaced by his father Joseph, a man of integrity, a man much blessed from his childhood by the God of heaven; a man whose fruitfulness, and divine blessings, life adversities could not stop (Genesis 49:22 – 26).

These new twelve-character types of the twelve tribes found in Revelation 7 summarize the various character groups which could be found in the human race; each human-being has a dominant of one of these characters, which symbolically identifies him to a specific name of a tribe of Israel; if one belongs to Christ, he is Abraham's seed, and heir according to the promise (Galatians 3: 29).

According to the book of Revelation, the New Jerusalem has twelve gates having the names of the twelve children of Israel. Regardless of his character type, if the sinner repents from his sins, and decides to live for Jesus, he will enter through one of those gates to the city of the New Jerusalem.

They are the first fruits: "…These were redeemed from among men, being firstfruits to God and to the Lamb" (Revelation 14:4-NKJV). A first fruit is the first or prime installment of a bigger number; in other words, the 144,000 are the specimen or representation or first quality of all saints; this means they represent all the redeemed of the earth; they are living witnesses of holiness, the quintessence of what it is to die to self and live for the glory of God; as the Levites were a kind of a special army of God among the children of Israel. If they are living saints, then all the redeemed dead in Christ are a symbolical representation of their number. In the book of Numbers 8: 16 -18 - NIV, of the Levites God said: "They are the Israelites who are to be given wholly to me. I have taken them as my own in place of the firstborn, the first male offspring from every Israelite woman. Every firstborn male in Israel, whether human or animal, is mine. When I struck down all the firstborn in Egypt, I set them apart for myself. And I have taken the Levites in place of all the firstborn sons in Israel". Also in (Numbers 8:14-NIV), it is written: "In this way you are to set the Levites apart from the other Israelites, and the Levites will be mine". If they are first fruits, and preachers of the final harvest, they must exist indeed to represent all the redeemed of all time. And if they are literal, the great multitude or those who await the first resurrection should then be the symbolical representation of the same number they are called by. They were not numbered among the Israelites; they represented the whole group. In Numbers 3, God said about them: "The Lord said to Moses in the Desert of Sinai, "Count the Levites by their families and clans. Count every male a month old or more. So Moses counted them, as he was commanded by the word of the Lord" (Numbers 3: 14-15-NIV). These verses clearly portray that they were counted and precisely numbered according to the instructions of the Lord (Numbers 3:39); but separately from the whole group; they well existed to represent all the children of Israel.

They come from a great tribulation: To behold Christ in all the adversities of the world seem to be the greatest challenge for the believers of today. How different will their time of trouble be from all the trouble the world is already witnessing? Today, Christ ever lives in the most holy place of the sanctuary to intercede for His children (Hebrews 7:25); for that reason we can come boldly to the throne of grace to receive mercy in time of need (Hebrews 4:16); this means, even amidst all the evil we see happening today, the grace of God is still a power that is restraining Satan to exercise all his power over us. But Christ intercession will not last forever; since His work in the most holy place is antitypical to the day of atonement of the sanctuary service in the wilderness, His work has an end, and will soon be over. At that time, darkness will cover the earth; all restraint on Satan, the enemy of souls will be removed; Jesus will no longer be interceding. To live without intercessor during that time and the great tribulation that will follow will not be a play. If Christ is not at that time living fully in the life of the believer, life will be difficult. But at that time, the 144000 will be able to make it, because they have learned in their lifetime obedience through sacrifice (Psalm 50: 2-3); they have learned in their lifetime what it is to deny self; and they will be able to survive because, they have not loved their own lives even unto death; they owe their life, their all to God. These people are those whom the world, the whole universe and the angels are waiting to see manifested for the final vindication of the character of God. They will be the fierce enemies of the devil and his angels and of the unrepentant sinners, because Jesus will be shining through them (Job 41: 30 – 32).

Their unity: Looking back at the Levites, Doukhan (2016) said: "What one learns from the Levites is that genuine fraternity and social cohesion begins with love for the stranger … the Levites allow for the true structure of interpersonal relationships to come to the fore". Of the skin of the Leviathan, it is said in Job 41 that "His rows of scales are his pride, shut up tightly as with a seal; one is so near another that no air can come between them; they are joined one to another, they stick together and cannot be parted (Job 41:15 -17-NKJV); the folds of his flesh are joined together; they are firm on him and cannot be moved (Job 41:23-NKJV).

- **They serve God day and night in the temple**: Peck, (2014) made the comment that the Levites while ministering in the earthly sanctuary, lodged around about the house of God" where they served day and night " I Chronicles 9:26,27,33; and so their successors the 144,000, will serve God "day and night in His temple." (Rev. 7:15).

-   About the Levites, it is said in the Bible (Deuteronomy 10:8 - NKJV): "At that time the Lord separated the tribe of Levi to bear the ark of the covenant of the Lord, to stand before the Lord to minister to Him and to bless in His name, to this day."

-   "The Levites had the job of helping Aaron's descendants in the service of the Lord's Temple. They also cared for the Temple courtyard and the side rooms in the Temple. And they made sure all the holy objects were kept pure. It was their job to serve in God's Temple. They were responsible for putting the special bread on the table in the Temple and for the flour, the grain offerings, and the bread made without yeast. They were also responsible for the baking pans and the mixed offerings. They did all the measuring. The Levites stood every morning and gave thanks and praise to the Lord. They also did this every evening. The Levites prepared all the burnt offerings to the Lord on the Sabbath days, during New Moon celebrations, and on the other special meeting days. They served before the Lord every day. There were special rules for how many Levites should serve each time. So the Levites did everything that they were supposed to do. They took care of the Holy Tent and the Holy Place. And they helped their relatives, the priests, Aaron's descendants, with the services at the Lord's Temple. "(1 Chronicles 23:28-32- ERV).

    So likewise in Revelation 7:15-NIV, it is said of the 144,000 : "Therefore, "they are before the throne of God and serve him day and night in His temple; and He who sits on the throne will shelter them with His presence".

-   **They have washed their robe and made them white**: signify they are justified by the blood of Jesus; they have fully accepted the justification of Jesus-Christ through faith; they realized their need of salvation as it was in Acts 2:37 – 38, Acts 4:12 and Acts 16:30. They have humbled themselves before God and have received His pardon. To wash one´s robe is one thing; but to make it white takes striving, suffering and bleaching; this means these special saints have not only fully accepted the righteousness of Jesus-Christ; but they have suffered all they could to keep their robe of righteousness spotless. They live to bear the fruits of regeneration; like Job, they have suffered for their faith in the most difficult time of life; the Holy Spirit has transformed their wicked heart into pure loving vessels bearing the fruits of the Holy Spirit: love, joy, peace, loving kindness, temperance, patience, compassion, mercy, goodness; these fruits are characters developed in the most difficult times of their life trials .

- In the Old Testament, the Levites wore white robes. In the book of Numbers, it is said of them: "The Levites purified themselves and washed their clothes. Then Aaron presented them as a wave offering before the LORD and made atonement for them to purify them" (Numbers 8:21-NIV).

- **They follow the Lamb everywhere**: This means leaving everything that could separate us from Jesus as did the first disciples who followed Jesus wherever He went during His ministry on earth. "The 144,000 as Special Witnesses. Among the redeemed a special witnessing will be given by the 144,000, and for this they receive special preparation. As the result of earnest, faithful, prayerful study of God's Word, this company have a pure faith, - "for they are virgins," Revelation 14:4, - " (Peck, 2014). They followed the Ark and live close to the sanctuary.

- Numbers 1:51-NASB: "So when the tabernacle is to set out, the Levites shall take it down; and when the tabernacle encamps, the Levites shall set it up. But the layman who comes near shall be put to death."

- Numbers 1:53-NASB: "But the Levites shall camp around the tabernacle of the testimony, so that there will be no wrath on the congregation of the sons of Israel. So the Levites shall keep charge of the tabernacle of the testimony."

- Numbers 8:19-NIV: "From among all the Israelites, I have given the Levites as gifts to Aaron and his sons to do the work at the tent of meeting on behalf of the Israelites and to make atonement for them so that no plague will strike the Israelites when they go near the sanctuary".

- (Job 41: 4-NKJV: "Will it make an agreement with you for you to take it as your slave for life?"

- Psalm 50:5-NIV: "Gather to me this consecrated people, who made a covenant with me by sacrifice."
    There was no guile found in their mouth. As it was discovered earlier, the tribe of Levi was known for the promotion of social cohesion, no backbiting between brothers. They do not divide each other; they unite as the united apostles during the descent of the Holy Spirit; in literal sense it could be said of them that they were the joined or coiled brothers described in the scales of the Leviathan. Likewise the 144,000 will constitute a strong united inseparable entity; Ellen . White commented saying: "The 144,000 were all sealed, and perfectly united. On their foreheads was written, "God, New Jerusalem," and a glorious star containing Jesus' new name (White, Review and Herald Articles, 1945).

- **Sealed, and perfectly united:** the Swiss theologian Louis Second (Second, 2010) translated Job 41 verse 17 "they are brothers who embrace each other, seize each other, and remain inseparable.

The Rising of the Leviathan in Job 41

The book of Genesis chapter 6, gives the principal reasons and the historical context which quickly led to the destruction of the antediluvians and their world; the heart of man was continuously turned to evil; in other words, there came a time when the imprint of the character of God could no longer be seen in the man He made in His image and for His glory. Man rather became known for his character without God; he became so wicked that if left alone in his evil doing, he would have plunged the whole universe in total chaos.

The book of Ezekiel 14:12 -17-NKJV gives a general idea of what brings God´s judgment on His people: "The word of the Lord came again to me, saying: "Son of man, when a land sins against Me by persistent unfaithfulness, I will stretch out My hand against it; I will cut off its supply of bread, send famine on it, and cut off man and beast from it. Even if these three men, Noah, Daniel, and Job, were in it, they would deliver only themselves by their righteousness," says the Lord God. "If I cause wild beasts to pass through the land, and they empty it, and make it so desolate that no man may pass through because of the beasts, even though these three men were in it, as I live," says the Lord God, "they would deliver neither sons nor daughters; only they would be delivered, and the land would be desolate. "Or if I bring a sword on that land, and say, 'Sword, go through the land,' and I cut off man and beast from it, even though these three men were in it, as I live," says the Lord God, "they would deliver neither sons nor daughters, but only they themselves would be delivered".

The time in which these three men of God lived were times of general apostasy; in the time of Job, people were drinking, killing, and stealing (Job 1: 15 18); on top of this, Job himself had a very difficult life; in the time of Daniel, Israel was taken captive to Babylon when the nation of Judah rebelled against God; they were carried to "a center of idolatry and one of the most wicked cities in the ancient world" (Walvoord, 2008); Evil in such terrible proportions was to bring God´s judgment in their times. But Noah, Job, Daniel were found faithful; God could count on them; He could trust them when none of His children was trustable; their personal relationship with God and commitment to Him brought them salvation in time of calamity.

Matthew Henry (Ezekiel 14:14 Commentaries, 2004) said "The faith, obedience, and prayers of Noah prevailed to the saving of his house, but not of the old world. Job's sacrifice and prayer in behalf of his friends were accepted, and Daniel had prevailed for the saving his companions and the wise men of Babylon. But a people that had filled the measure of their sins, was not to expect to escape for the sake of any righteous men living among them". In other words, the situation in which these men of God lived in, gave a wake-up call for the longing and thirst of God´s righteousness to be reestablished on earth; and their lives accounted just for that.

Now to talk about the work of the Leviathan, it will be fair to consider the faithfulness of the tribe of Levi during the time Israel committed what has been known in history as the greatest scandal of the wilderness. During that time, bull worship was common in the Ancient Near East (Tigay, 2003); Tigay believed that Aaron wished to build a calf in honor of God for the people who asked for it; but their intention portrayed an idol in replacement of Moses as a mediator of God´s presence; clearly, they did not intend to have a calf to depict God, but an idol that functioned among them as Moses did. The Levites did not take part in this idol worship during all these apparent silence of God´s presence. After the incident, they were set apart:

- "You have been set apart to the LORD today, for you were against your own sons and brothers, and he has blessed you this day " (Exodus 32:29)-NIV.

Today, while we have involved the world in sins that were not even known in the time when God destroyed entire nations, God seems ever silent. Men have defied Him by making sin religiously acceptable. But He is patient toward Mankind longing for men to repent (2 Peter 3:9). The question that Moses asked the people when he came down from Mount Sinai was: "who is on the Lord side?-Exodus 32-26-KJV" Unlike these patriarchs, this final vindication of God´s character will involve the whole human race; like the Levites at Sinai, those thirsty of righteousness and holiness, those who want to live wholly consecrated for God, those who are willing to pay the price of self-denial are the ones that will be able to stand unshakable in the time of trouble such as never before. They are the Levites of the last days, or Leviathan. They will be God´s final answer:

- To Job´s questionings about suffering (Job 3:8)
- To the whole universe;(Romans 8:21)
- To Satan (Job 1:9)

Their commitment will solve the final issue of obedience; even when Jesus stepped out between man and God, when Satan is given all his power, their loyalty to God will be the same. Why were they so specially singled out? "Because they had to stand with a wonderful truth right before the whole world, and receive their opposition, and while receiving this opposition they were to remember that they were sons and daughters of God, that they must have Christ formed within them the hope of glory (MS 13, 1888)." "These are they which came out of great tribulation; they have passed through the time of trouble such as never was since there was a nation; they have endured the anguish of the time of Jacob's trouble; they have stood without an intercessor through the final outpouring of God's judgments" (White E., 1990).

God's Marking before the General Destruction: The Sealing

God's marking or protection during the time of trouble is the sealing; it is a sheltering God provides for His children to ensure they are safe during the destruction time; examples of this:

- Before his calamities, Job was sealed by God (The Lord said to Satan, "Very well, then, he is in your hands; but you must spare his life.- Job 2:6-NIV)

- Before the destruction of Jerusalem the early Christians found refuge in the city of Pella (Wilson, 2012)

- Before the final destruction in Egypt the Israelites were protected by sprinkling blood-mark on the doorpost of their houses to ensure the protection of their first born.(Exodus 12)

- Ezekiel was shown the same sealing in vision in the 9th chapter of his book; a sealing which is to take place before the general destruction on earth; this sealing begins in the house of God; but continues outside the house of God, since Jesus does not only have children in His house (the church), but also many outside He will bring in. About this, Jamieson and R, & David (1871) commented that "when all things else on earth are confounded, God will secure His people from the common ruin. He will make sure they are kept safe before He orders the punishment of the rest."

- The 144,000 will have already been provided a shelter before passing in the trouble.

- The authorship of Psalm 91 has been long discussed by Bible scholars. Without a certain name or date of composition, it is yet believed this Psalm was written by Moses because of its content that speaks about historical events supposedly relating to the plagues in Egypt. The Psalm gives an idea of what kind of shelter the sealing will represent to the children of God during those time of trouble similar to the ten plagues of Egypt. The Bible tells in the book of Revelation that the redeemed of the Lord will sing the song of Moses and of the Lamb; it is the song of the experience they would have gone through; this experience is not limited to the events related to the crossing of the Red Sea; the red sea became the focal point where the armies of Egypt used their last power to retain Israel captive; but were defeated by Jehovah, the God of Heaven. Israelites have themselves witnessed the troubles the plagues have brought upon the land of Egypt before their departure; their safety was found in the shelter of the arms of God alone; Psalm 91 supposedly written by Moses give us an idea about this sealing or shelter:

- *He who dwells in the secret place of the Most High Shall abide under the shadow of the Almighty. I will say of the Lord, "He is my refuge and my fortress; My God, in Him I will trust." Surely, He shall deliver you from the snare of the fowler. And from the perilous pestilence. He shall cover you with His feathers, and under His wings you shall take refuge; His truth shall be your shield and buckler. You shall not be afraid of the terror by night, nor of the arrow that flies by day, nor of the pestilence that walks in darkness, nor of the destruction that lays waste at noonday. A thousand may fall at your side, and ten thousand at your right hand; But it shall not come near you. Only with your eyes shall you look, and see the reward of the wicked. Because you have made the Lord, who is my refuge, Even the Most High, your dwelling place, no evil shall befall you, nor shall any plague come near your dwelling; For He shall give His angels charge over you, to keep you in all your ways. In their hands they shall bear you up, lest you dash your foot against a stone. You shall tread upon the lion and the cobra, the young lion and the serpent you shall trample underfoot. "Because he has set his love upon Me, therefore I will deliver him; I will set him on high, because he has known My name. He shall call upon Me, and I will answer him; I will be with him in trouble; I will deliver him and honor him. With long life I will satisfy him, and show him My salvation"(NKJV).*

The sealing is done by the Holy Spirit (Ephesians 4:30). It precedes the four winds. In the Bible, since it began in Revelation 6, after the opening of the 7 seals, it is important to review these seals or stages of the Christian church from the early church to the time of the religious awakening in the 1700s.

- The first seal of Revelation 6 or white horse, symbolizes the victorious apostolic church, or historical time of the church of Ephesus (A.D. 30-100);

- The second seal of Revelation 6 or red horse, symbolizes the church under Roman persecution. Its historical time corresponds to that of the church of Smyrna; (AD 100 – 313);

- The third seal of Revelation or Black horse, symbolizes the apostate church. Its historical period corresponds to that of the church of Pergamos (AD 313 - 600);

- The fourth seal of Revelation 6 or Pale horse, corresponds to the reformation period and Papal rulership. Its historical period corresponds to that of the church of Thyatira (AD 600- 1517);

- The fifth seal corresponds to the post reformation period; Martyrs were under the altar. Its historical period was that of the church of Sardis (1517 – 1755);

- The sixth seal talks about cosmic disturbances (falling of the stars), the dark day; it was also the time of spiritual awakening of the 1800 with great revivals, missionary movement all across America and Europe; its historical period was that of the church of Philadelphia; according to David L. Rowe (Nichol, 2013), during those days, many Millerites looked through natural phenomena (powerful thunderstorms light, eclipses) to find signs of the soon return of Jesus Christ, and of the end of the world; and they believed (according to Ruth Alden) that Jesus Christ was about to appear in the skies of heaven.

Bible verses	Symbolisms	The seals of Revelation 6	The 7 churches	Church Periods
Revelation 6 : 1- 2	White horse	First seal	Ephesus	AD 30 -100
Revelation 6 : 2 - 4	Red horse	Second seal	Smyrna	AD 100 -313
Revelation 6 : 5 - 6	Black horse	Third seal	Pergamos	AD 313 -600
Revelation 6 : 7 - 8	Pale horse	Fourth seal	Thyatira	AD 600 -1517
Revelation 6 . 9 - 11	Post Reformation	Fifth seal	Sardis	AD 1517 -1755
Revelation 6 : 12- 14	Signs of the Second coming	Sixth seal	Philadelphia	AD 1800

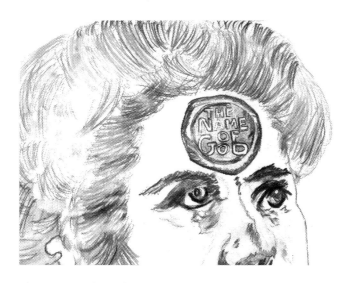

The first attempt

These seals of Revelation 6 portraying the seven stages of the Christian church were not independent from the events that followed in Revelation chapter 7. The events of Revelation 7 marked the beginning of the sealing of the saints. After the events of Revelation 6, Revelation 7 introduced four angels standing in the four corners of the earth, "holding the four winds of the earth, that the wind should not blow on the earth, on the sea, or on any tree"(Revelation 7:1)-NKJV. In Revelation 7:2, another angel was ascending from the East with the seal of the living God, crying to the four angels not to harm the earth, the sea until the living saints or 144,000 were sealed; in other words, Revelation 7 verses 1 and 2 talk about the beginning of the sealing of the saints which directly followed the opening of the seven seals in the previous chapter (Revelation 6).

This sealing which began in the 1800 did not end; the angels did not release the winds of strife and the time of trouble did not come at that time. Talking about the winds of strife of Revelation 7, Ellen White (White E. G., 2012) wrote: "Men in responsible positions will not only ignore and despise themselves, but from the sacred desk, will urge upon the people the observance of the first day of the week, pleading tradition and custom in behalf of this man-made institution. They will point to calamities on land and sea—to the storms of wind, the floods, the earthquakes, the destruction by fire—as judgments indicating God's displeasure because Sunday is not sacredly observed." In other words, the winds of strife to be let go by the angels relate to the national Sunday law or mark of the beast; in the time when she was writing, she believed sealing was in progress; she wrote (White E. G., Early Writings, 1945): "Satan is now using every device in this sealing time to keep the minds of God's people from the present truth, and cause them to waver. I saw a covering that God was drawing over His people to protect them in the time of trouble; and every soul that was decided on the truth, and was pure in heart, was to be covered with the covering of the Almighty"; and in 1885, she wrote (White E. G., Christian Services, 1947): "We are standing on the very verge of the Eternal World".

To receive this seal of God, we must accept Jesus-Christ fully; and the Sabbath is the sign that Christ dwells or abides in the life of the believer. Talking about this character of Christ in the life of the believer, AT Jones (1893) wrote:

- The Sabbath being the sign of what Christ is to the believer, will the believer know fully what the Sabbath is until he knows fully what Christ is? [Congregation: "No."] So then when the knowledge of God in Jesus Christ has absorbed all of the mind itself, then the Sabbath will be also known fully to the mind itself. But the Sabbath is the sign of what God is in Christ, and when that is brought fully to the mind itself, what is that but the image of God, the name of God, in the mind of the believer, and that the seal of the living God, through the Sabbath of the Lord."

Regarding this seal of God, (Prescott, 1893) made this very important declaration as well;

- " …only in so far as Christ is seen in the Sabbath is the Sabbath a seal. But the Spirit is the agency by which we are transformed by the renewing of our minds, that Christ may be formed within. Now when the Sabbath is recognized as the institution of Christ, and that Christ is the very essence of the Sabbath, do you not see that when the Sabbath is properly and really kept in the spirit of it, that it is when Christ is received in his fullness?"

In other words, the seal of God lies in the fact that Jesus is the Lord of the Sabbath and through the Sabbath, He through His grace impresses His character into us. Sabbath keeping without character change does not give the seal. But accepting God's grace and keeping the Sabbath impresses the seal into us like the seal leaves a mark on wax or paper.

The event in history which could be pointed out to as far as a National Sunday Law is concerned was the Blair Bill (Co, 1889) of May 21, 1888; this was proposed in the American congress; but this Bill was not passed, below is the copy of the Bill:

NATIONAL SUNDAY-REST BILL
SENATE BILL No. 2983, INTRODUCED IN FIRST SESSION OF FIFTIETH CONGRESS, BY SENATOR H. W. BLAIR, MAY 21, 1888. BILL TO SECURE TO THE PEOPLE THE ENJOYMENT OF THE FIRST DAY OF THE WEEK, COMMONLY KNOWN AS THE LORD'S DAY, AS A DAY OF REST, AND TO PROMOTE ITS OBSERVANCE AS A DAY OF RELIGIOUS WORSHIP.

Be it enacted by the Senate and House of Representatives of the United States of America, in Congress assembled, That no person or corporation, or the agent, servant, or employee of any person or corporation, shall perform or authorize to be performed, any secular work, labor, or business, to the disturbance of others, works of necessity, mercy, and humanity excepted; nor shall any person engage in any play, game, or amusement, or recreation, to the disturbance of others, on the first day of the week, commonly known as the Lord's day, or during any part thereof, in any territory, district, vessel, or place, subject to the exclusive jurisdiction of the United States; nor shall it be lawful for any person or corporation to receive pay for labor or service performed or rendered in violation of this section.

SECTION 2. That no mails or mail matter shall hereafter be transported in time of peace over any land postal route, nor shall any mail matter be collected, assorted, handled,

or delivered during any part of the first day of the week:
Provided, That whenever any letter shall relate to work
of necessity or mercy, or shall concern the health, life, or
decease of any person, and the fact shall be plainly stated
upon the face of the envelope containing the same, the
Postmaster-General shall provide for the transportation
of such letter or letters in packages separate from other
mail matter, and shall make regulations for the delivery
thereof, the same having been received at its place of
destination before the said first day of the week, during
such limited portion of the day as shall best suit the public
convenience and least interfere with the due observance
of the day as one of worship and rest: And provided
further, That when there shall have been an interruption
in the due and regular transmission of the mails, it shall
be lawful to so far examine the same when delivered as
to ascertain if there be such matter therein for lawful
delivery on the first day of the week.

SECTION 3. That the prosecution of commerce between the
States and with the Indian tribes, the same not being work
of necessity, mercy, nor humanity, by the transportation
of persons or property by land or water in such way as to
interfere with or disturb the people in the enjoyment of the
first day of the week, or any portion thereof, as a day of rest
from labor, the same not being labor of necessity, mercy, or
humanity, or its observance as a day of religious worship,
is hereby prohibited; and any person or corporation, or the
agent or employee of any person or corporation, who shall
willfully violate this section, shall be punished by a fine of
not less than ten nor more than one thousand dollars; and
no service performed in the prosecution of such prohibited
commerce shall be lawful, nor shall any compensation be
recoverable or be paid for the same.

SECTION 4. That all military and naval drills, musters,
and parades, not in time of active service or immediate

preparation therefor, of soldiers, sailors, marines, or cadets of the United States, on the first day of the week, except assemblies for the due and orderly observance of religious worship, are hereby prohibited, nor shall any unnecessary labor be performed or permitted in the military or naval service of the United States on the Lord's day.

SECTION 5. That it shall be unlawful to pay or to receive payment or wages in any manner for service rendered, or for labor performed, or for the transportation of persons or of property in violation of the provisions of this act, nor shall any action lie for the recovery thereof; and when so paid, whether in advance or otherwise, the same may be recovered back by whoever shall first sue for the same.

SECTION 6. That labor or service performed and rendered on the first day of the week in consequence of accident, disaster, or unavoidable delays in making the regular connections upon postal routes and routes of travel and transportation, the preservation of perishable and exposed property, and the regular and necessary transportation and delivery of articles of food in condition for healthy use, and such transportation for short distances from one State, District, or Territory, into another State, District, or Territory, as by local laws shall be declared to be necessary for the public good, shall not be deemed violations of this act, but the same shall be construed, so far as possible, to secure to the whole people rest from toil during the first day of the week, their mental and moral culture and the religious observance of the Sabbath day.

Robert J. W (Wieland) said that the message of the righteousness of Christ rejected in the 1888 was "the starting point of the long-awaited latter rain and of the loud cry spoken about in Revelation 18; if accepted, the gospel commission would have ended in 1893; so "something must have gone wrong", since 100 years after, we are still waiting for the loud cry. Revelation 7 verses 1 to 3 (NKJV) explains well this scenario that happened at that time: "Then I saw another angel ascending from the East, having the seal of the living God. And he cried with a loud voice to the four angels to whom it was granted to harm the earth and the sea, saying, "Do not harm the earth, the sea, or the trees till we have sealed the servants of our God on their foreheads".

This righteousness by faith in Christ message is the message that prepare the children of God for the sealing and the translation that will follow: (Ellen W. G., 1900) wrote : "Christ is waiting with longing desire for the manifestation of Himself in His church. When the character of Christ shall be perfectly reproduced in His people, then He will come to claim them as His own". So since this message of the righteousness of Christ was rejected, the sealing did not continue, the Sunday Law was not passed, the four winds were not released; because the children of God did not accept the character of Christ to be fully reproduced in them so they could be sealed before the winds are released; the righteousness of Christ is the main ingredient of the sealing; as it was rejected, God in His grace did not let the wind blow, because His children were not ready.

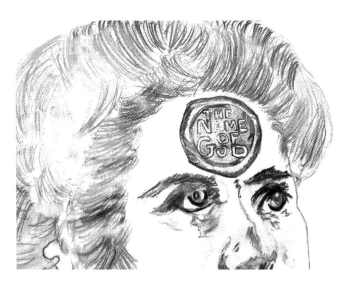

The second sealing

There is a second mention of the 144,000 found in Revelation 14; in Revelation 14, the 144,000 stand ; the Greek word translated to stand in this verse is the word "histemi", which means: place, set up, establish, appoint; set in balance, I stand, stand by, stand still; met: to stand ready, to stand firm, to be steadfast (Lockman D., 1981). In the context of this verse this second time, the 144,000 now stand firm, or ready, steadfast and established. Ellen White (Ellen W. G., 1900) in Christ object Lessons said : "God will not allow the four angels to release the four winds of the earth until He is certain that He can develop 144,000 loyal saints (Revelation 14:12) in one generation. Christ will come when the 144,000 are fully developed." All are to come from one generation. So far, all Christians have tried with the best of their ability to follow the Lord; but these people will behold the character of Jesus totally, without mistake; they will be totally surrendered to Jesus-Christ.

A People Ready for the Kingdom of God

Once being asked by the Pharisees when the kingdom of God would come, Jesus replied: "And when he was demanded of the Pharisees, when the kingdom of God should come, he answered them and said: "The kingdom of God cometh not with observation, "Neither shall they say, lo here! or, lo there! for, behold, the kingdom of God is within you (Luke 17:20 -21 - KJV)". What it will take for the kingdom of God to be manifested, is people who are willing to deny self and allow Jesus to fill them with the Holy Spirit; once these people are found, the kingdom of God will be manifested on this earth and the end will come. It is interesting to notice that right after Jesus made this statement He spoke about:

- The end of probation: "Then He said to the disciples, the days will come when you will desire to see one of the days of the Son of Man, and you will not see it". (Luke 17 verse 22- Berean Study Bible), "They ate, they drank, they married wives, they were given in marriage, until the day that Noah entered the ark, and the flood came and destroyed them all (Luke 17: 27)-NKJV.

- The great deception and the time of trouble: "And they will say to you :'Look here!' or 'Look there! 'Do not go after them or follow them. For as the lightning that flashes out of one part under heaven shines to the other part under heaven, so also the Son of Man will be in His day. But first He must suffer many things and be rejected by this generation. And as it was in the days of Noah, so it will be also in the days of the Son of Man"- Luke 17:23- 25-NKJV),

The availability of the empty vessels to be filled with the Holy Spirit is what God is waiting for. The manifestation of these shining saints marks the end of Christ intercessory work in the heavenly courts. Here will be fulfilled the words of Jesus :" You are the light of the world. A city that is set on a hill cannot be hidden. Nor do they light a lamp and put it under a basket, but on a lampstand, and it gives light to all who are in the house. Let your light so shine before men, that they may see your good works and glorify your Father in heaven "(Matthew 5:14 – 16-NKJV). With their holy life the 144,000 will enlighten the world with the glory of God. These shining saints:

- Will be the sons of God who will have as Father the God Creator of heaven and earth;
- Will only live to do the will of God as did Jesus their Lord;
- Will live only to glorify the name of God;
- Will long for the soon establishment of the kingdom of God on earth;
- Will serve God as did Job, Enoch, Daniel and Noah;
- Will be miraculously taken care of by God every day; and that will be enough for them to trust God for every day; in times when they will not have, they will still trust Him; of them after their trials, the Bible said "They shall neither hunger anymore

nor thirst anymore; the sun shall not strike them, nor any heat" (Revelation 7:16-NKJV).
- Will be sheltered by God before the plagues.
- Will not retaliate when the wicked will try to harm them; because of Christ living in them, they will peacefully forgive;
- will cry out to God day and night for deliverance;
- will behold the return of Jesus in His glory; shout of triumphs will come out of their mouth, for their deliverance have come :" Thine is the Kingdom, the power and the glory.

This kingdom life is recorded in the book of Matthew 6:9 -13. The disciples saw the mighty works of Christ during His days. They concluded that He was successful after spending hours in prayer. They asked Jesus to teach them how to pray. To answer their request, He gave them what we have commonly known as the Lord´s prayer; that prayer was a summary of how the disciples of Jesus were to live the kingdom life for the kingdom of God to shine on this earth. It summarizes the lifestyle yet to be lived by true Christians on this earth; but the day is soon coming when this prayer will be the life and essence of those who will vindicate the character of God; here it is:

- Our Father in heaven,
- hallowed be Your name,
- Your kingdom come,
- Your will be done,
  on Earth as it is in Heaven.
- Give us this day our daily bread,
- And forgive us our debts,
  as we also forgive our debtors.
- And lead us not into temptation,
- But deliver us from evil the evil one.
- For Yours is the kingdom, and the power, and the glory, forever, Amen (NKJV).

The Lord's Prayer	The Leviathan in time of trouble
Our Father, who art in heaven	*Then I looked, and there before me was the Lamb, standing on Mount Zion, and with him 144,000 who had his name and his Father's name written on their foreheads (Revelation 14:1).*
Hallowed be thy Name	*These are those who did not defile themselves with women, for they remained virgins. No lie was found in their mouths; they are blameless- (Revelation 14: 4 -5)* Those that overcome the world, the flesh, and the devil. will be the favored ones who shall receive the seal of the living God" (White, 1966).
Thy kingdom come	Servants of God, endowed with power from on high. with their faces lighted up, and shining with holy consecration, went forth to proclaim the message from heaven. (White, 1945)
Thy will be done *on earth as it is in heaven*	Darkness thickened around them; yet they stood firm, approved of God, and trusting in Him ... Day and night their cry ceased not: "Thy will, O God, be done! (White, 1945)
Give us this day our daily bread.	Bread and water is all that is promised to the remnant in the time of trouble.— (White, 1870).
And forgive us our trespasses, as we forgive our debtors	The righteous, in their distress, will have a deep sense of their unworthiness, and with many tears will acknowledge their utter unworthiness, and like Jacob will plead the promises of God through Christ, made to just such dependent, helpless, repenting sinners (White, 1945)

The Lord's Prayer	The Leviathan in time of trouble
And lead us not into temptation, but deliver us from evil.	*It was an hour of fearful, terrible agony to the saints. Day and night they cried unto God for deliverance. To outward appearance, there was no possibility of their escape. The wicked had already begun to triumph, crying out, "Why doesn't your God deliver you out of our hands? Why don't you go up and save your lives?" But the saints heeded them not ... For His name's glory He would deliver every one of those who had patiently waited for Him and whose names were written in the book. It was at midnight that God chose to deliver His people. As the wicked were mocking around them, suddenly the sun appeared, shining in his strength, and the moon stood still. The wicked looked upon the scene with amazement, while the saints beheld with solemn joy the tokens of their deliverance* (White, 1945)
For thine is the kingdom, and the power, and the glory, for ever and ever. Amen.	*... The Israel of God stood with their eyes fixed upward, listening to the words as they came from the mouth of Jehovah and rolled through the earth like peals of loudest thunder. It was awfully solemn. At the end of every sentence the saints shouted, "Glory! Hallelujah!" ... No language can describe the glory of the scene. The living cloud of majesty and unsurpassed glory came still nearer, and we could clearly behold the lovely person of Jesus ...* (White, 1945)

The Leviathan and the Time of Trouble

There are two different events in the Bible that can help us have an idea about the time of trouble: the trial of Jesus, and the trial of Job.

The Trial of Jesus: This trial began in the garden of Gethsemane. When Jesus was praying, He saw the cup He was about to drink for Mankind to be saved; He fell on His face. Then He said to them, "My soul is exceedingly sorrowful, even to death. Stay here and watch with Me. He went a little farther and fell on His face, and prayed, saying, "O

My Father, if it is possible, let this cup pass from Me; nevertheless, not as I will, but as You will." (Matthew 26:38-39-NKJV). Jesus was carrying the sins of all sinners upon Himself. How serious is this? Sorrowing over one sin and its consequences can be mentally destructive; what if it is not one sin, but two or three? Here, Jesus was not to carry one sin of a sinner; but all the sins from the birth to the death of every human being all together at once from the beginning to the end of time. This was one of the darkest moments of earth. He was arrested; He began the road of agony alone because of love. He went from one courtroom to the other; He was beaten, He was slapped in the face, He was hungry, He lost His friends, He was insulted, He was mocked by the crowd He fed, He carried the cross. He was nailed on that cross while carrying all the sins, the guilts, shame, condemnation of every single human being. During that time, His Father kept silent; the angels kept silence; the world He came to save became His enemy. This is one example of the time of trouble. But as Pilate looked in His face, he saw God; he saw the stillness of One who was ready to go through the adversity filled with the Spirit of God (White, 1898)

The Trial of Job: Job one day, without paying for the price of any wrong he has done, began to lose his children one after the other, his properties, his belongings, everything that made him who he was; he lost them all; his friends accused him of sin amidst adversity; his wife and closest companion asked him to curse God and die; he was left alone. As Job faced the trials, he did not curse God; instead he responded to the trials saying that, even if his skin is totally destroyed he will see God (Job 19:26). He faced the trials having the Spirit of God in Him.

These are the pictures of what a time of trouble really looks like; lonely hours with mental, physical, emotional and spiritual anguishes. The trials of Job and the trial of Jesus as He came to take our place in judgment, summarize in themselves the definition of the great controversy between God and Satan; Those are what we should keep in mind if we don't know well what definition we can give to the time of trouble.

When Jesus finished His work on earth, talking about Satan He said, " ...the ruler of this world is coming, He has nothing in Me" (John 14:30-NKJV). When Jesus will finish His work of intercession in the heavenly courts and the time would have come for the Prince of this world to manifest his evil power on earth, he will have nothing in the children of God to claim for himself; for they will be filled with the Spirit of Jesus. When Jesus will leave the intercession of the Most Holy place, there will be no more intercession for the sinner; the time of grace would have ended; the Holy Spirit of God will no longer be pleading with the guilty sinner; darkness will cover the earth as the devil and his angels will be loosed to exercise their power to the fullest; unrepentant sinners will be responsible for their sins since birth. It will be a terrible time. When Jesus finished His ministry and was about to go to the cross (Mark 15:51- 53), in those darkest hours of the middle of the night, a young man, wearing nothing but a linen garment, was following Him. When the soldiers seized him, he fled naked, leaving his garment behind; that garment is the symbol of the righteousness of Christ or our mantle of protection during the darkest hours of earth; in other words, if we do not have Jesus living inside of us before the time He finishes His work, we will be left without covering before the time of trouble; Jesus said: "Look, I come like a thief! Blessed is the one who stays awake and remains clothed, so as not to go naked and be shamefully exposed" (Revelation 16: 15-NIV); "I counsel you to buy from Me gold refined in the fire, that you may be rich; and white garments, that you may be clothed, that the shame of your nakedness may not be revealed"(Revelation 3:18-NKJV). Ellen G White (1945) said that those who receive the seal of the living God and are protected in the time of trouble must reflect the image of Jesus fully.

Regarding the plagues before the time of trouble and the end of the world, Ellen. G White wrote :

- "It was impossible for the plagues to be poured out while Jesus officiated in the sanctuary; but as His work there is finished, and His intercession closes, there is nothing to stay the wrath of God, and it breaks with fury upon the shelterless head of the guilty sinner, who has slighted salvation and hated reproof. In that fearful time, after the close of Jesus' mediation, the saints were living in the sight of a holy God without an intercessor. Every case was decided, every jewel numbered." (White E. G., The Story of Redemption, 2002).

- "When Jesus leaves the sanctuary, then they who are holy and righteous will be holy and righteous still; for all their sins will then be blotted out, and they will be sealed with the seal of the living God. But those that are unjust and filthy will be unjust and filthy still; for then there will be no Priest in the sanctuary to offer their sacrifices, their confessions, and their prayers before the Father's throne. Therefore what is done to rescue souls from the coming storm of wrath must be done before Jesus leaves the most holy place of the heavenly sanctuary." (White, 1945).

Christ in you, The Hope of Glory

One of the most important characteristics of the 144,000 is that they come out of a great tribulation. In Revelation 7:16-NIV, it is written:

- Never again will they hunger; never again will they thirst. The sun will not beat down on them,' nor any scorching heat. For the Lamb at the center of the throne will be their shepherd; 'He will lead them to springs of living water. "And God will wipe away every tear from their eyes."

This implies they have gone through indescribable trials before the return of Jesus.

The Work of Suffering

When God made Man, He never intended for him to suffer. He made Man to be happy. God did not want Adam and Eve to experience suffering. But the devil made them believe that through disobedience their eyes will be opened; It was through this lie that Adam and Eve knew what God did not want them to know: suffering. In the life of Job as well, God did not intend his servant to suffer; it is Satan who, when he was permitted, used suffering to make the life of Job a misery: "And the Lord said unto Satan, Behold, all that he hath is in thy power; only upon himself put not forth thine hand" (Job 1:12-KJV).

Suffering is Satan's most important tool to destroy and discredit the holy and loving character of God. In suffering, when man is faced with trouble and pains, he tends to concentrate on his problem, he ignores God or blame Him for his misfortune. This gives Satan opportunities to question God's love and mock His name.

Suffering in Redemption

But God did not leave Man at the mercy of Satan to be destroyed. When Man sinned, God needed to redeem him. In God's plan to redeem Man, Jesus-Christ His Son took upon Himself the suffering that was to be the lot of Man, providing Man a way of escape. Jesus-Christ was the Lamb slain from the foundation of the world, the Lamb provided by God, the Passover Lamb, and the Lamb of God that takes away the sins of the world (Genesis 3:21; Genesis 22:7-8;1 Corinthians 5:7; John 1:29). By the exemplar life that Jesus-Christ lived through the trials He suffered, Man has hope to overcome and be reunited with God. In Hebrews 5: 8,9 (NIV), it is written of Jesus: "Son though He was, He learned obedience from what He suffered and, once made perfect, He became the source of eternal salvation for all who obey Him". In his trials, if his eyes are fixed on Jesus who is his hope of deliverance, Man's sinful dispositions are changed and purified into holy dispositions and into a holy character. Through this process, the presence of God is to reappear in the life of the transformed sinner. Paul call this presence of Christ in the life of a believer "a mystery among the gentiles"(Colossians 1:27); an example of this is the presence of God in the life of Daniel in Babylon (Daniel 5:11,

14). With this, it can be said that the difficulties and trials that make the life of Man a misery are used for his good, as "part of the training needful in God's plan for his uplifting from the ruin and degradation that sin has wrought" (White, 2000).

The purification Process of the 144,000: This purification in the life of the Leviathan or those who will vindicate the name of God in the last days is spoken about in the book of Malachi: "And he shall sit as a refiner and purifier of silver; and he shall purify the sons of Levi, and purge them as gold and silver, that they may offer unto the Lord an offering in righteousness". Barnes (1870) said: "But more largely, as Zion and Jerusalem are the titles for the Christian Church, and Israel who believed was the true Israel, so "the sons of Levi" are the true Levites, the Apostles and their successors in the Christian priesthood". Theodore (1645) said, "God begins at the priests, that they might be lights, and shine unto others". This suggests that this is a special group of Levites whose work will be to shine unto others; Daniel also who himself had the Spirit of Christ in him spoke about this group of people: "Those who are wise will shine like the brightness of the heavens, and those who lead many to righteousness, like the stars for ever and ever". Using the purification of silver to describe this God's cleansing process of the saints spoken about in the book of Malachi 3, W. H. Lewis (1905 -1909) wrote: "During the earlier stages of the process, the film of oxide of lead, which has constantly remained over the melted surface of the mass, is removed as rapidly as can be, and the color of the metal is dark; but when the silver is almost clear of impurities, the film of litharge upon its surface grows finer and finer, and a succession of beautiful rings, of iridescent tints, form, one after another, until at last the film of oxide suddenly melts away and disappears, and the brilliant surface of the silver flashes forth in all its purity and glory. Under the old methods, the watcher did not disturb the crucible until that last change came, until he could see his own image on the glowing surface. Then his work was done, and his purpose fulfilled. Charles F. Deems, D. D (Joseph, 1905 -1909) affirmed this thought by saying: "When Christ sees His own image in His people, His work of purifying is accomplished. Then He instantly removes the crucible from the fire". And Ellen White (1900) also spoke about this: "When the character of Christ shall be perfectly reproduced in His people, then He will come to claim them as His own". This was a reference to the purification of the special type of Levites of the last days or the Leviathan in Job 41, namely the 144000.

Character Perfection: Perfection does not mean the state of sinlessness, but Christian character maturity developed through trials. Ellen G White (1990) said: "We should seek to become perfect in Christ ... this is the condition in which those must be found who shall stand in the time of trouble". An example of this kind of perfection was Job himself. Of him, it is said in Job 1:1-NKJV "There was a man in the land of Uz, whose name was Job; and that man was perfect and upright, and one that feared God, and eschewed evil". In his trials, Job was perfect, but he was not sinless; this means he was patient in trial, enduring in suffering and faithful to God.

The purpose of the trials of the Leviathan (or 144,000), and supposedly for every child of God, is for them to master their struggles, attain emotional stability, emotional health, and character maturity, which will allow them to be conformed to the image of Christ. The things we hold on to so dear do not and will not give us true satisfaction but leave us empty and void; the more we fill our heart with these earthly things, the emptier and more sorrowful we become; and the more we will need something more satisfying for our soul. But only Jesus can satisfy a soul in the real sense. When His Holy Spirit comes in the believer, He progressively lessens our interests for things which do not have eternal values. He first subdues the sinful affections and lusts of the flesh as Paul said in Galatians 5:24 and 25-NIV: "Those who belong to Christ Jesus have crucified the flesh with its passions and desires. Since we live by the Spirit, let us keep in step with the Spirit". The final goal is for the sinful affections to die for the heart to be filled with love, patience, kindness, joy, peace, longsuffering, gentleness, goodness, faith, meekness, temperance developed through adversity. This means the sinful desires in our lives that separate us from God are given up for the sake of Christ to the point of becoming living sacrifices for Jesus.

Talking about this group of people, Ellen G White (2004) wrote: "It's needful for them to be placed in the furnace of fire. Their earthliness must be consumed for the image of Christ to be reflected". This level of perfection is the one every true believer in Christ is to have before trying times.

Self-denial, Key Condition for Christ Living in us: In His answer to Job, God used the character symbols of the crocodile to teach lessons of self-denial and total submission. The final words of Job 41 proved this:

- He beholds every high thing. Benson (1846) made the following comment: "Here ends the words of God to Job. Whereby he sets forth his wisdom and power in the works of the creation: from whence Job might be let to infer that the wisdom and power of God being so immense, men ought to speak so reverently of Him and think most humbly of themselves; persuaded that though we cannot always see the reason why the divine providence suffers certain things to come to pass, yet we ought to rest assure that they are wisely, and therefore justly, ordered, and therefore we should resignedly submit ourselves to the divine will in all things".

- Gill (1999) said : "But be the Leviathan what it may, it certainly is an illustrious instance of the power of God in making it; and therefore Job and every other man ought to submit to Him that made it, in all things, and be humble under his mighty hand; owning freely, that it is his right hand, and his only, and not man's, that can save, either in a temporal or spiritual sense.

To be king over a situation or a "kingdom" is to have authority, supremacy, dominion or power over them. The Leviathan is said to be king over all the children of pride; it surpasses all that is called pride; in the context of Job 41, he has overcome pride and he has power over it.

Our personal freedom is linked to a severe divine training needed for greater responsibilities in God´s universe tomorrow.

Denying self to follow Jesus makes us loose what is precious for the temporal gratification of the flesh. The process is painful and sorrowful; because it makes us undergo God´s fiery cleansing that leads unto holiness. When the Spirit of God is working in the life of the believer, when the believer is tried and shaken, washed in the hands of his Maker for the sake of God´s kingdom, he sometimes experiences weariness, wound and heavy pains; but as he humbly allows himself to be fashioned in faith and total surrender by yielding his will to God´s authority, he allows God´s transforming power to change him, mold him and reshape him into the holy image of Jesus-Christ. The attributes of the Holy Spirit of God begin to replace the works of the flesh until Christ and Christ alone begins to be seen in him and lives in him. His contrite and humble heart becomes a living temple of God (Isaiah 57:15). This was the very desire of Jesus: "I in them, and You in Me; that they may be made perfect in one, and that the world may know that You have sent Me and have loved them as You have loved Me" (John 17:23-NKJV).

Practical Christianity advice from the apostle of Jesus-Christ. To have such a close connection with God, our spiritual preparation is needed in these last days. James the brother of Jesus, Peter, and the apostle Paul gave advice on what believers are to do to have such a closer walk with God. James wrote in his Gospel 1:4-NKJV: "But let patience have its perfect work, that you may be perfect and complete, lacking nothing". In addressing the believers persecuted by Nero in his lifetime, James the brother of Jesus sent a more specific end-times message; his message was addressed to the twelve tribes scattered among the nations; he emphasized the righteousness by faith message; he spoke of believers faith in trial and of the eternal reward; he said that God "Of His own will He brought us forth by the word of truth, that we might be a kind of firstfruits of His creatures"(James 1:18-NKJV); and he made mention of the early and the latter rain.

James´ encouragement was for believers to live a life that will bring forth the manifestation of the sons of God, or Leviathan for the final vindication of God´s name. He called for Christians to have a Christlike character more important than outward experience; a character tried through hardship and rejection, to count it all joy in order to develop godly patience, to avoid a spirit of envy, self-seeking and friendship with the world, and a pure Christian heart which implies godly speech, a teachable spirit, compassion for the less fortunate, and the same consideration for everyone.

Paul in Ephesians 4 calls for believers to live in peace and with honesty with everyone by avoiding all malice and evil speaking,

speaking the truth in love, living away from anger and bitterness, having a forgiving heart, a humble and gentle spirit, being patient and tenderhearted toward one another as Christ our Lord, constantly connected to God through prayer, and having the mindset of the soon return of the Lord Jesus.

Peter exhorts believers to watch over what they say, to be thankful to God in everything, to be heavenly minded and heavenly bound.

The Making Up of the Leviathan

llen White (1900) in the book Christ Object Lesson wrote: "God will not allow the four angels to release the four winds of the earth until he is certain that He can develop 144,000 loyal saints (Revelation 14:12) in one generation. Christ will come when the 144,000 are fully developed". In the book Great Controversy (1990), she wrote: "Jesus would be honored by translating, without them seeing death, the faithful, waiting ones who had so long expected Him". In Revelation 14:4-5-NKJV, we read: "These are the ones who were not defiled with women, for they are virgins. These are the ones who follow the Lamb wherever He goes. These were redeemed from among men, being first-fruits to God and to the Lamb. And in their mouth was found no deceit, for they are without fault before the throne of God". In the book of Numbers 8:15 to 19 (NIV) as seen earlier, of the Levites it is said: "After you have purified the Levites and presented them as a wave offering, they are to come to do their work at the tent of meeting. They are the Israelites who are to be given wholly to me. I have taken them as my own in place of the firstborn, the first male offspring from every Israelite woman. Every firstborn male in Israel, whether human or animal, is Mine. When I struck down all the firstborn in Egypt, I set them apart for Myself. And I have taken the Levites in place of all the firstborn sons in Israel. From among all the Israelites, I have given the Levites as gifts to Aaron and his sons to do the work at the tent of meeting on behalf of the Israelites and to make atonement for them so that no plague will strike the Israelites when they go near the sanctuary". In Numbers 2:33-NIV, it is written: "The Levites, however, were not counted along with the other Israelites, as the Lord commanded Moses". In Numbers 3: 11-13 (NIV), the Lord also said to Moses, "I have taken the Levites from among the Israelites in place of the first male offspring of every Israelite woman. The Levites are Mine, for all the firstborn are Mine. When I struck down all the firstborn in Egypt, I set apart for myself every firstborn in Israel, whether human or animal. They are to be Mine. I am the Lord". And in Numbers 3: 15-16-NIV: "Count the Levites by their families and clans. Count every male a month old or more." So, Moses counted them, as he was commanded by the word of the Lord".

The Levites in the Old Testament were very well numbered according to the instructions of God given to Moses; they were taken in replacement of the first born of the children of Israel from the twelve tribes; but they were not numbered together with Israel as a whole. They existed in a specific number, and as a representation of all the children of Israel before God. In the Old Testament, they existed in literal number and as a symbolical entity for the whole nation of Israel. The Leviathan in the book of Job, the 144,000 are types of the tribe of Levi as seen so far.

God chose the Levites in the Old Testament for a specific work to do. Throughout the Bible in time of apostasy, the remnant of God´s people has always been, but a small number.

According to Jewish source during the Passover, only one fifth of the Jews left Egypt; the other 80% perished in Egypt during the last plague (Suchard, 2005), (Kirshblum, 2004)

- In the time of the destruction of Jericho, only Rahab and her family were saved (Joshua 5:25);
- When God was looking for warrior to fight the Midianites, out of 32000 people, only 300 people were ready (Judges 7).
- When Israel built the golden calf in the wilderness, only Moses and the Levites remained faithful to God (Exodus 32:25);
- When God was to destroy Sodom and Gomorrah, only Lot and his children were saved (Genesis 19);
- During the Babylonian captivity, only Daniel and his friends remained faithful to God (Daniel 2).
- Even though Noah preached to the world in his time, his message was not welcomed, and only him and his family were saved (Genesis 7).

Even though the people of the Lord are like the sand by the sea, only a remnant will return, said the Word of God in Isaiah 10:22. Living in the sight of a holy God without Mediator will require genuine Christianity. For that reason, our commitment for the Lord today should be a total consecration;

Special resurrection?

It is believed by some Christians today that there will be a special resurrection before the first resurrection of the death; this special resurrection will happen during the proclamation of the third angel message of Revelation 14, and that those who will be raised from that resurrection will be part of the 144,000. The basis or biblical verse used for this argument is Daniel 12: 1-2-NKJV- "And at that time your people shall be delivered, everyone who is found written in the book. And many of those who sleep in the dust of the earth shall awake, some to everlasting life, some to shame and everlasting contempt".

Daniel 12:1 to 3 summarizes the events of the end of time: the close of probation, the time of trouble coinciding with the seven last plagues, the Second Coming of Christ and the establishment of His everlasting kingdom. Daniel 12:3 especially speaks of the wise who will shine like the brightness of the heavens, and lead many to righteousness like the brightness of the stars. This verse is an implicit description of the sons of righteousness described in Romans 8:19, the 144,000 or Leviathan in Job 41. Their work as seen in the previous chapter will be to shine on others like the stars in the night in the darkest hours of earth history.

The events of Daniel 12 verses 1 to 3 however are not in chronological order. According to the order in which the verses appear, Daniel the prophet spoke of:

- The close of general probation;
- There shall be a time of trouble;
- The final deliverance of the saints;
- Resurrection of righteous and unrighteous;
- Rising of the sons of God or sons of righteousness.

Since the events are not in chronological order, the biblical principle of interpretation found in Isaiah 28:10 can be applied to reconstruct the whole scene (Isaiah 28:10: For precept must be upon precept, precept upon precept; line upon line, line upon line; here a little, and there a little); this principle is applicable for example for the metaphor of the story of redemption puzzled in the Song of Solomon.

With proper order, the events in Daniel 12:1 - 3 would be as followed:

- Rising of the sons of righteousness;
- Close of general probation(Michael shall stand).
- The time of trouble;
- The final deliverance of the saints;
- Resurrection of righteous and unrighteous;

Regarding these two resurrections spoken about in Daniel 12 verse 2, the following comment can be read on Amazing Discoveries (Heritage, 2010): "The words *"shall awake"* here speak of the resurrection of the dead. The righteous at the glorious Second Coming of Christ are raised to meet their Redeemer and receive life everlasting. The wicked dead will be raised later to receive their reward". This implies that like Paul in 1 Thessalonians 4 verses 15 -17, and like John in Revelation 20 verses 5 – 8, Daniel was also speaking about only two mains resurrections at the return of Jesus: one of the righteous and the one of the unrighteous.

For that reason, in this book, to be in line with the Scriptures as a whole and reconcile with the writings of Paul and John the Revelator, we will conform to these two resurrections only.

We leave the rest to the wisdom of the Almighty God, to the time when He will unfold everything and make all things plane for the world to see at His return.

Give God the Instruments and He Will Finish the Work

At the cross, God has given an opened demonstration of His love before the whole universe, so man may freely see the truth and choose whom he wants to serve (Colossians 2:15). Every human being is a sinner who has fallen short of the glory of God (Romans 3:23; Romans 3: 11 – 12). God calls every human to come to Him just as he is, so all may be freely justified (Romans 3:24); not to stay the same but to allow Him to work in our lives, so He might from day to day transform us into the holy image of Jesus-Christ His Son.

Talking to His disciples before His supreme sacrifice on the cross, Jesus said: "And this gospel of the kingdom shall be preached in all the world for a witness unto all nations; and then shall the end come"- Matthew 24:14-KJV. According to Lockman (1998), the word "witness" comes from the word *"Martus"* (from which came the word martyr). The 144,000 would have never seen Jesus; yet they are His living witnesses;

they have made a covenant with God through sacrifice (Psalm 50:5); for their lives are proofs of their experiential relationship with God. They are His living witness because their will has been subdued to the authority of the Holy Spirit. The song of their experience is the song of their relationship with Jesus as of Paul in Acts 16:6 - 10; they have a genuine experience with Jesus-Christ.

For the Gospel work to finish in the world, God needs available human instruments who will allow Him to finish the work in them first. His eyes "run to and fro throughout the whole earth, to show Himself strong on behalf of those whose heart is loyal to Him (2 Chronicles 16:9-NKJV). At last, He will use the Leviathan of Job 41 to finish the work and *"cut it short in righteousness"*. Paul call them the remnants, long awaited Sons of God; Malachi called them God´s precious jewels; the psalmist called them God´s army:

- "Though the number of the children of Israel be as the sand of the sea, the remnant will be saved. For He will finish the work and cut it short in righteousness, because the Lord will make a short work upon the earth" (Romans 9:27-28-NKJV).

- "They shall be Mine, says the Lord of hosts, on the day that I make them My jewels. And I will spare them as a man spares his own son who serves him." Then you shall again discern between the righteous and the wicked, between one who serves God and one who does not serve Him (Malachi 3:17-18-NKJV).

- "Your troops will be willing on your day of battle. Arrayed in holy splendor, your young men will come to you like dew from the morning's womb" (Psalm 110:3-NIV).

They are the specimen that are to forever stand before God to represent all the saved throughout earth history. Only heaven knows the individuals who are to compose this group called the Leviathan in Job 41 or the 144000. In 1 Corinthians 4:5 (NIV), it is written "Therefore judge nothing before the appointed time; wait until the Lord comes. He will bring to light what is hidden in darkness and will expose the motives of the heart. At that time each will receive their praise from God". In line with this passage of the Scriptures, Ellen White (1958) wrote: "It is not His will that they shall get into controversy over questions which will not help them spiritually, such as who is to compose the hundred and forty-four thousand. This those who are the elect of God will in a short time know without question".

But anybody can be part of this wonderful group of people. All we need, is the power of the cross, or that willingness to surrender all to Jesus who gave all for us that we might have eternal life. The attitude of Paul is our best example in this. When he was seized by the love of Jesus, by the cross, he said: "What is more, I consider everything a loss because of the surpassing worth of knowing Christ Jesus my Lord, for whose sake I have lost all things. I consider them garbage, that I may gain Christ ..." (Philippians 3:8-NIV); "for Christ's love compels us, because we are convinced that one died for all, and therefore all died. And He died for all, that those who live should no longer live for themselves but for Him who died for them and was raised again" (2 Corinthians 5:14 -15-NIV); "I am crucified with Christ: nevertheless I live; yet not I, but Christ lives in me: and the life which I now live in the flesh I live by the faith of the Son of God, who loved me, and gave himself for me" (Galatians 2:20-KJV). Knowing the price ahead, Paul encouraged every believer to give it all to Jesus for the sake of the kingdom. In Romans 12:1 the advice of Paul is for the Christians to understand the importance of offering ourselves to God as living sacrifices; for there is no other way Christ could come to live in us and fill us with His presence if we do not offer ourselves to Him; for that is the true, reasonable and intelligent way of worship or Christian service.

Heaven is waiting for empty vessels to be filled with the Holy Spirit of God; the universe has been long waiting for the children of righteousness to shine for the glory of God. Let us give God the instruments as Job, Daniel, Noah, Paul and the disciples of Christ did. Who is on the Lord's side Moses asked? As the Levites answered, let us stand for God, let us give him the instruments, so He might finish the work. By His grace we can.

End Words

Eternity will matter for all the sacrifices we do today to glorify the name of Jesus. It is high time to allow God to work in us; it is high time to have an experiential relationship with Jesus-Christ; it is high time to give God permission to purify us and finish the work in us (Revelation 3:20). Paul said the universe is still waiting for the manifestation of the sons of God. Daniel gave God the instrument, Job gave God the instrument, Noah gave God the instruments. If we give God the instruments, He will finish the work.

Give God the instrument, and He will finish the work!

> May your prayer be:
> Lord, all that I have, all that I am,
> I offer You as a living sacrifice;
> All that I need, is all of You;
> Give me all that You have;
> Your Holy Presence to live in me,
> So that I shine for the glory of Your name.
> May you be God´s answer for the final battle;
> May you be part of the Leviathan for the glory of God;

Give God the instruments, and He will finish the work.
In Jesus name. Amen!

Heaven will be for those who desire it with intense desire, who put forth efforts in proportion to what they seek (White 1952)

Let us give God the instruments and He will finish the work.

References

Alligator. (n.d.). Retrieved from Britannica Kids Students: https://kids. britannica.com

Angier, N. (2004). Not Just Another Pertty Face. *New York Times*.

Barnes, A. (1870). *Study Light*. Retrieved from Commentry on Malachi 3:3: www.studylight.org

Be Crocwise. (n.d.). Retrieved from Department Of Envoronment And Heritage Protection (Queensland Government): https://www.ehp. qld.gov.au

Benson, J. (1846). *The Holy Bible containing The Old And New Testament with Critical Explanatory And Practical Notes*. New York: G. Lane & C.B. TIPPETT.

Benson, J. (1857). *"Commentary on Job 3:8". Joseph Benson's Commentary*. Retrieved from Study Light: www.studylight.org

Benson, J. (1857). *Study Light*. Retrieved from Verse-by-Verse Bible Commentary Job 41: www.studylight.org

Britton, A. (2012). *Crocodilian Biology Database*. Retrieved from Crocodilian: http://crocodilian.com

Brown, F. (1906). *Hebrew And English Lexicon Of The Old Testament*. Oxford: Clarendon Press.

Brown, J.-F. (n.d.). *Job 3 Jamieson Fausset Brown Bible Commentary*. Retrieved from Bible Hub: www.biblehub.com

Bunch, T. g. (1997). *Exodus And Advent Movements in Type and Antitype*. Brushton: Teach Services.

Cam, L. (2014, March 6). *Top 10 Animals That Can Survive Without Food*. Retrieved from Top 10 List Land: http://www. top10listland.com

Campbell, J. (1738). *A New And Complete History Of The Old Testament.* London: Horace's Head.

Campbell, L. (n.d.). *The Leviathan:A Transformation.* Retrieved from Academia: www.academia.edu

Charles, H. (1913). *"Levites" Catholic Encyclopedia.* New York: Robert Appleton Company.

Co, P. P. (1889, February 15). Sunday Rest Bill. *The Sentinel Library,* p. 12.

Coffman, J. B. (1983). *Coffman's Commentaries on the Bible.* Retrieved from Study Light: www.studylight.org

Coffman, James Burton. (1999). *Coffman Commentaries on the Old and New Testament.* Abilene: Ablene Christian University Press.

Coke, T. (1801-1803). *Commentary on Job 41:32 .* Retrieved from Study Light: www.studylight.org

Doukhan, A. (2016). *Biblical Portraits of Exile: A philosophical reading.* Routledge: Abingdon, Oxon.

Ellen, G. W. (1903). *Education: The Lifework .* Montain View, CA : Pacific Press Publishing Association.

Ellen, G. W. (1913). *The Writing and Sending Out of the TEstimonies to the Church.* Mountain View, CA: Pacific Press Publishing Association.

Ellen, G. W. (2007). *Lucifer, How art Thou Fallen.* Brushton: Teach Services.

Ellen, W. G. (1900). *Christ's Object Lessons.* Nampa: Pacific Press Publishing.

Farbiarz, R. (2009, February 16). *MISHPATIM.* Retrieved from American Jewish World Services: https://ajws.org

Finkel, A. (1993). *Essence f the Holy Days: Insight from The Jewish Sages.* New York: Jason Aronson.

Gerety, R. M. (2018). *Go Tell The Crocodiles in Mozambique.* New York: New Press.

Giblett, R. (2009). *Landscapes of Culture And Nature.* Hampshire: Palgrave MacMillan .

Gill, J. (1999). *"Commentary on Job 3:8". "The New John Gill Exposition of the Entire Bible.* Retrieved from Study Light: www.studylight.org

Gill, J. (1999). *Commentary of Job 41:1.* Retrieved from Study Light: https://www.studylight.org

Gill, J. (1999). *The New John Gill's Exposition of the Entire Bible Commentary On Genesis 49:16.* Retrieved from Study Light: www.studylight.org

Gill, j. (n.d.). *Job 41.* Retrieved from Bible Hib: www.biblehub.com

Ginzberg, L. (1909). *The Legends of The Jewish Vol III.* Philadelphia: Jewish Publication Society.

Hardinge, L. (2012). *Stones of Fire.* Hagerstown: Review And Herald Publishng.

Hawn, C. M. (1938). *History of Hymns: "Precious Lord, Take My Hand".* Retrieved from Discipleship Mnistries: https://www.umcdiscipleship.org

Hays, J. (2008). *Crocodiles: Their History, Characteristics And Behaviour.* Retrieved from Facts And Detais: http://factsanddetails.com

Henry, M. (1706). *Job 41.* Retrieved from Bible Study Tools: www.biblestudytools.com

Henry, M. (2004). *Ezekiel 14:14 Commentaries.* Retrieved from Bible Hub: www.biblehub.com

Heritage, F. (2010). *Daniel 12 KJV Commentary.* Retrieved from Amazing Discovery: www.amazingdiscoveries.org

Jamieson, R. D., R, F. A., & David, B. (1871). *Commentary on Ezekiel 9:4.* Retrieved from Study Light: www.studyliht.org

Job 41:12. (2011). Retrieved from Studylight.org: https://www.studylight.org

Jones, A. (1893). The Seal and The Sabbath. *General Conference Bulletin/General Conference Daily Bulletin,* 455.

Joseph, E. (1905 -1909). *Malachi 3:3 Commentaty.* Retrieved from Study Light: www.studylight.org

Kirshblum, R. J. (2004, February 03). *Questions to Ponder.* Retrieved from Torah.org: www.torah.org

Lockman. (1998). *NAS Exhaustive Concordance of the Bible with Hebrew And Aramaic And Greek Dictionaries.* Retrieved from lockman.org: www.lockman.org

Lockman, D. (1981). *2476.Histemi.* Retrieved from lockman foundation: www.lockman.org

Matthew Black, H. H. (1962). *Peake commentary of The Bible.* Scotland: Thomas Nelson.

Ministerial Association, General Conference of Seventh Day Adventist . (1997). *Communion With God: To see His face.* Silver Spring, MD: Pacific Press Publishing Association .

Morris, H. (2000). *The Remarkable Record Of Job.* Green Forest: Master Books.

Mulzac, K. D. (1997). *Praying with Power* . Huntsville, AL: Beka Books .

Nichol, F. D. (2013). *Midnight Cry.* Fort Oglethorpe: Teach Services.

Peck, S. (2014). *The Path To The Throne Of God.* Fort Oglethorpe: Teach Service.

Poole, M. (1685). *"Commentary on Job 3:8".* Matthew Poole's English *Annotations on the Holy Bible.* Retrieved from Study Light: www. studylight.org/commentaries/mpc/job-3.html

Prescott, W. (1893, February 24). The Seal And The Sabbath. *General Conference Daily Bulletin,* p. 388.

Ross, H. (2014). *Hidden Treasures in the book of Job.* Ada: Baker Books.

Schwartz, R. H. (2001). *Judaism And Vegetarianism.* New York: Lantern Books.

Second, L. (2010). *La Sainte Bible.* Philadelphia: American Bibl Society.

Sherstha, T. K. (2001). *Herpetology of Nepal: A Field Guide For Amphibians and Rptiles of Trans-Hymalayan Region of Asia.* Nepal: Bimala Sherstha.

Singer, I. (1907). *Jewish Encylopedia.* New York: Funk & Wagnalls .

Singer, I. (2016). *The Jewish Encyclopedia: 1906 Edition.* Seattle: Amazon Digital Services LLC.

Spurgeon, C. H. (2011). *Commentary on Isaiah 27:4".* "Spurgeon's *Verse Expositions of the Bible.* Retrieved from Study Light: www. studylight.org

Suchard, R. Z. (2005). *Direction.* Jerusalem: Feldheim Publishers.

Surridge, R. (1991, June). *The Beast From the Earth.* Retrieved from Ministry Magazine: www.ministrymagazine.org

Team, A. (2014, July 17). *Crocodiles can go for years without eating anything.* Retrieved from World Of Animals: https://www. animalanswers.co.uk

Team, A. A. (2014, July 17). *Crocodiles can go for years without eating anything.* Retrieved from World Of Animals: https://www. animalanswers.co.uk

The Edinburg Review of Critical Journal. (1844). New Yror: Leonard Scott & Co.

Theodore, B. (1645). *Commentary on Malachi 3:3.* Retrieved from Study Light: www.studylight.org

Thiele, E. R. (1946). The Seven-headed Beast of Revelation. *Ministry Magazine*, 1.

Tigay, J. H. (2003). *The JPS Torah Commentary: Deuteronomy.* Arch Street : The Jewish Publication Society;.

Trapp, J. (1865). *John Trapp Compete Commentary.* Retrieved from Study Light: www.studylight.org

Traut, E. (n.d.). *SELECTED WORD-STUDIES OF NEW TESTAMENT GREEK WORDS.* Retrieved from New Testament Words: www.ntwords.com

Van der Toorn, van der Horst, Pieter, Becking. (1999). *Dictionary of Deities and Demons in the Bible.* Eerdmans Publishing.

Walvoord, J. F. (2008, January 1). *Early Life Of Daniel In Babylon.* Retrieved from Bible.org: www.bible.org

Waters, T. (n.d.). *Tribe of Levi:History, Symbol and Descendants.* Retrieved from Study.com: www.study.com

Wesley, J. (1765). *Wesley's Explanatory Notes.* Retrieved from Study Light: www.studylight.org

White, E. (1990). *The Great Controversy.* Nampa: Pacific Press.

White, E. G. (1889, March 19). *The Review And Herald.* Retrieved from EGW Writings: https://m.egwwritings.org

White, E. G. (1898). *The Desire of Ages.* Mountain View, CA: Pacific PRess Publishing Association.

White, E. G. (1943). *Prophets and Kings.* Nampa: Pacific Publisher.

White, E. G. (1945). *Early Writings.* Hagerstown: Review and herald publishing association.

White, E. G. (1945). *Review And Herald Articles.* Tellico Plains: Digital Inpiration.

White, E. G. (1947). *Christian Services.* Hagerstown: Review And Herald Publishing Associattion.

White, E. G. (1952). *My Life Today.* Hagerstown: Review And Herald.

White, E. G. (1958). *Selected Messages.* Hagerstown: Review And Herald Publishing Association.

White, E. G. (1966). *The Crisis Ahead*. Angwin: Robert W. Olson Pacific Union College.

White, E. G. (2000). *Steps To Christ*. Nampa: Pacific Press Publishing Assocation.

White, E. G. (2002). *Patriarchs And Prophets*. Nampa: Pacific Pr Pub Assn.

White, E. G. (2002). *The Story of Redemption*. Hagerstown: Review And Herald Publishing Association.

White, E. G. (2004). *To Be Like Jesus*. Hagerstown: Pacific Press Publishing Association.

White, E. G. (2011). *Testimonies For the Church Vol 9*. North Charleston: cREATESPACE.

White, E. G. (2012). *Signs of The Times Articles*. Tellico Plains: DDigital Inspiration.

Wieland, R. j. (n.d.). Lightened With His Glory. *The Gospel Herald*, www.gospel-herald.com.

Wilson, M. (2012, July 16). *Pella: A Window on Survival*. Retrieved from Biblical Archeology Society: www.biblicalarchaeology.org

Printed in the United States
By Bookmasters